# The Next Threat

D1736205

# Transnational Institute Series

The Transnational Institute is an independent fellowship of researchers and activists living in different parts of the world, who develop innovative analyses of world affairs.

It serves no government, political party or interest group.

## Other titles available in the TNI series:

**Short Changed:**
Africa and World Trade
*Michael Barratt Brown and Pauline Tiffen*

**People and Power in the Pacific:**
The Struggle for the Post-Cold War Order
*Walden Bello*

**Dark Victory:**
The United States, Structural Adjustment
and Global Poverty
*Walden Bello*

**Beyond Bretton Woods:**
Alternatives to the Global Economic Order
*Edited by John Cavanagh, Daphne Wysham
and Marcos Arruda*

**The Debt Boomerang:**
How Third World Debt Harms Us All
*Susan George*

**Pax Americana?**
Hegemony or Decline
*Jochen Hippler*

**Bonn & the Bomb:**
German Politics and the Nuclear Option
*Matthias Küntzel*

For information about forthcoming titles in this series contact Pluto Press

# The Next Threat

**Western Perceptions of Islam**

## Edited by Jochen Hippler and Andrea Lueg

**Translated by Laila Friese**

Pluto  Press
with
**Transnational Institute (TNI)**

First published 1995 by Pluto Press
345 Archway Road, London N6 5AA
and 5500 Central Avenue
Boulder, Colorado 80301, USA
in association with
the Transnational Institute (TNI),
Paulus Potterstraat 20, 1071 DA, Amsterdam

British Library Cataloguing in Publication Data
A catalogue record for this book is available from the British Library

Library of Congress Cataloging-in-Publication Data
The Next Threat. English.
    The next threat: Western perceptions of Islam / edited by Jochen
Hippler and Andrea Lueg; translated by Laila Friese.
        p.   cm.   — (Transnational Institute series)
    Includes bibliographical references (p.   ) and index.
    ISBN 0-7453-0954-2
    1. Islamic countries—Foreign public opinion, European. 2. Islam—
Public opinion. 3. Public opinion—Europe.   I. Hippler, Jochen.
II. Lueg, Andrea, 1962–   . III. Friese, Laila. IV. Title.
V. Series.
DS35.74.E85F4513    1995
909'.0097671—dc20                                                    94-43473
                                                                          CIP

ISBN 9780745309538 softback
ISBN 0745309534 softback
ISBN 9780745309545 hardback
ISBN 0745309542 hardback


Designed and produced for Pluto Press by
Chase Production Services, Chipping Norton, OX7 5QR
Typeset from disk by Stanford DTP Services, Milton Keynes
Printed on demand by Antony Rowe Ltd, Eastbourne

# Contents

*Introduction* Jochen Hippler and Andrea Lueg     1

1   **The Perceptions of Islam in Western Debate**     7
    *Andrea Lueg*

2   **From Romanticisation to Colonial Dominance:
Historical Changes in the European Perception
of the Middle East**     32
    *Petra Kappert*

3   **How Medieval is Islam? Muslim Intellectuals
and Modernity**     57
    *Reinhard Schulze*

4   **'Islam is in Danger': Authority, Rushdie and the
Struggle for the Migrant Soul**     71
    *Fred Halliday*

5   **Islam and Politics in the Middle East**     82
    *Azmy Bishara*

6   **The Islamic Threat and Western Foreign Policy**     116
    *Jochen Hippler*

7   **Conclusion: Dealing with Islam**     154
    *Jochen Hippler and Andrea Lueg*

*Notes on Contributors*     159
*Index*     161

# Introduction

*Jochen Hippler and Andrea Lueg*

Ideologues from East and West are enjoying a vogue. In almost all forms of the media, 'experts' seek to enlighten us on the new dangers from the East: holy wars, fanatical masses, the revenge of the Middle Ages on modernity and of religion on the Enlightenment. Islam is sometimes a 'challenge', sometimes a threat. The conquest of Vienna by the Turks is apparently once again imminent. With Khomeini, Gaddafi, Saddam Hussein, Arafat and the Algerian fundamentalists, the anti-Western wave is rolling on, at any rate splashing across popular magazines and television screens. The threat might be a spiritual one, an Oriental counter-model to Western civilisation; it might result in stopping the flow of oil, or in a cultural invasion by immigrants from Turkey or the Maghreb. It might lie in the Islamic atom bomb, in terrorism or in a threatened Islamic fundamentalist world revolution in the Iranian mould. Simple minds might even see it as a battle of Islam against Christianity, or against 'unbelievers'. In Europe and the USA all these perceptions of threats exist, sometimes side by side and at other times separately. Sometimes they crop up suddenly and compete with each other, and at other times they are systematised and compounded, all depending on what is required or desired in a particular situation.

This book will not examine Islam, but the West's hostile view of Islam (or the perceived 'Islamic threat'). It is a book about our own 'Western' way of thinking, about the need for, and the structure and consequences of, a Western view of Islam. One of our theories is that the current vogue for popular literature about the Islamic threat has little to do with the supposed threat itself – Islam – and more to do with Western thinking, with a lacuna in our identity due to the end of the Cold War. It is this aspect that interests us.

We are not, then, concerned with revealing 'the true Islam', by creating hostile or romanticised images of it. The societies of the Middle East that were shaped by Islam have many aspects that are very unpleasant and even threatening.[1] Although these phenomena threaten the people of the Middle East itself first and foremost, and not those of Europe and North America, this is by no means any reason

1

to take them lightly or to ignore them. We have as little sympathy or 'understanding' for Islamist–inspired acts of intolerance and fanaticism directed against Arabs, Turks or Persians, as we do for attacks by German skinheads on the German homeless and disabled, on Turkish or Lebanese girls or on anyone else. In neither instance, however, do we think that demonstrative hysteria is the right way to react.

When we criticise the perception of Islam as 'the enemy', we do so not in order to justify all aspects of Middle Eastern politics and society, or to sweep them under the carpet of 'cultural difference'. Rather, we highlight the fact that popular constructs of 'the enemy' are not a serious way of confronting oppression, contempt for women, abuses of human rights and other such phenomena. But these are precisely not what the ideologues who weave these hostile images are concerned with. Rather, they and their 'followers' are concerned with making themselves feel good by associating these problems with another culture and region. Instead of critique we have arrogance and schematism: we are against the fanaticism which is an integral part of another culture; fanaticism does not belong to the core of 'Western-Christian culture', it only sometimes emerges as a regrettable exception. Instead of criticising the faults in our own societies, and using the same yardsticks in their criticism of other societies, many authors set the two cultures against each other. In January 1992, the semi-official German weekly *Das Parlament* even went so far as to contrast the Islamic countries with 'the free world'. 'The free world' – that means us. This way of thinking is the theme of this book, a way of thinking that professes to fight foreign irrationality through European enlightenment while doing precisely the opposite: reverting to the pre-Enlightenment schemata which it is supposedly challenging. Often, even the patterns of argument of Islamists are taken on, dealing yet another blow to the liberal Muslims or secular intellectuals of the Middle East.

By contrast, we think that dismantling the construct of 'the enemy' does not signify lack of criticism but is a prerequisite for serious critique. To criticise self-constructed schemata does not constitute critique but demagogy. After all, it is realities that must be analysed, not fantasies.

In a recent article Bassam Tibi asked: 'Is Islamic fundamentalism an invention of Western strategists, who need a new "enemy"? This is what some German intellectuals apparently believe.' Tibi claims to have observed that 'many German moralists see any criticism of fundamentalism as an attempt to create new images of "the enemy" to replace the loss of communism'.[2]

Of course Islamic fundamentalism is no invention of Western strategists.[3] Even European and American intellectuals know this much. Apart from the fact that it never was an *invention*, it obviously originated in the Middle East. As mentioned above, there is much to be criticised about this unpleasant phenomenon, yet this obvious fact does not hinder Tibi's 'Western strategists' from exploiting an imagined Islamic threat. His arguments finally amount to this: fundamentalism is bad, therefore we must not criticise its critics. By contrast, we argue that although fundamentalism is bad, its critics are not automatically good, and some may well have ulterior motives.

Unlike serious criticism, a perceived threat means having to make a choice between two opposing sides. Instead of differentiating or analysing you only have to *choose* between two quite distinct alternatives. Critical analysis is thus replaced by an act of ideological faith.

In this book, we will henceforth refrain from constantly 'legitimising' our criticism of Western patterns of thinking, by periodically and ritually distancing ourselves from fundamentalism and Islamist movements. We think that they must be confronted politically – but that is not the subject of this book, even though at least two chapters make some suggestions on how this might be done.

In early 1993 an Egyptian journalist wrote:

This past month has brought fresh reminders of the West's double standards. The attacks against the supposed nuclear facility in Iraq show that there is no debate when it comes to the question of enforcing UN resolutions against a Muslim state; the point of discussion is merely one of interpretation, and about how far the West can go militarily. On the other hand, the Palestinians deported from Israel show that when UN resolutions are on behalf of Muslims, they carry little more weight than the paper they are printed on. These events have for now overshadowed the debate on Bosnia. But the primary point about each of these three cases is the same: the victimisation of Muslims by the West, which feeds radical Islam and undermines the ground of political moderates.[4]

This brings up a crucial point: Islamism, Islamic political religiosity, 'fundamentalism' (terms that are used synonymously in this book, and are seen in contrast to Islamic orthodoxy, popular religion or religious traditionalism) spring from the political, social and economic experiences of people in the Middle East. Whoever wishes to weaken them would be well advised to think first about how to solve the real problems of the region. To evade this need and to construct instead a stereotyped notion of 'the enemy' and grumble about the 'national character of the Arabs' or Muslims is no more rational or 'enlightened' than wanting to explain the attacks on refugee centres by reference to 'the national character of the Germans'.

The idea of an Islamic threat is nothing new. It has deep historical roots that date back as far as the Crusades which, as is well known, were invariably accompanied by anti-Semitic pogroms.[5] In the 1970s, following the oil price crisis of 1973 ('The Oil Sheikhs Are Turning Off Our Oil Supplies'), and a little later in the context of the Islamic Revolution in Iran, the issues were heavily emotionalised. This was also the case during the period of aeroplane hijackings by Palestinians, although sentiments then were marked more by anti-Arab/anti-Palestinian than religious feeling. As a result of the end of the Cold War, the perceived Islamic threat has, however, acquired a particularly explosive power in the 1990s. We no longer have the Soviet Union or communism to serve as enemies justifying expensive and extensive military apparatuses. It was in the mid-1980s at the very latest that the search began for new enemies to justify arms budgets and offensive military policies, at first as part of the communist threat and then in its place. First the 'War on Drugs', the somewhat absurd and naturally failed attempt to solve New York's drug problem by naval manoeuvres off the coast of South America and military operations in Bolivia, then 'Terrorism', a term applied to real terrorists as well as to various unpleasant freedom movements in the Third World which (of course) demanded military responses, were two such attempts during the 1980s. And as with the 'Islamic (or fundamentalist) threat' today, then too there were enough good reasons to be against drug dealers and terrorists. Neither of these social evils was ever fought seriously at its roots. Instead, they were exploited for other purposes. At that time the aim was to legitimise the newly developed doctrine of *low-intensity warfare*; today it is to justify high military expenditure when the traditional enemy has disappeared and we are objectively no longer threatened by conventional war. Fundamentalism, then, has not been invented by Western politicians, but is being used by them.

In this sense, making Islam into 'the enemy' (as opposed to having a real one) only contributes to the fact that a pivotal opportunity, the end of the Cold War, is being wasted. Now, given the loss of the old military opponent, instead of reducing the military apparatus in the West to a symbolic vestige or getting rid of it altogether and thinking about 'security' completely afresh, new threats are being invented to serve the old purpose. *This* is our main problem, not an

Islamic fundamentalist threat which, in any case, could only be dealt with by political and economic means.

In the first chapter of this book Andrea Lueg takes a look at the international media and examines central elements of their stereotyped image of Islam and the Islamic threat, and discusses how such perceptions arise and how they function. Following this, Petra Kappert examines the changes in Europe's view of the Orient from the French Revolution to the First World War. In this period, the perception of the Orient moved from unrealistic romanticisation to the arena of European superpower politics. Reinhard Schulze tackles the widely held theory that Islamic societies can have little connection with modernity at all, or can only achieve it by adopting the European model. His chapter deals mainly with the debate on modernity among Muslim intellectuals. Fred Halliday analyses the diversity of Muslim communities in Europe and relates it to the struggle inside the Islamic world. He thinks that this internal conflict between a rational and a dogmatic self-interpretation by Muslims will be of greater importance than any intercultural dispute. Azmy Bishara discusses the problems of stereotyping Islam, especially as regards fundamentalism and the theory about the unity of politics and Islam in the Middle East. He demonstrates that it is possible to analyse Islamist movements instead of just labelling them. Finally, Jochen Hippler examines the attitudes of Western foreign policy towards Islam and its fundamentalist variations, and establishes that more is involved than mere reflex actions to the current fears and perceptions of threat.

## Notes

1   In some of the chapters in this book the terms 'Islamic countries' and 'Islamic societies' are used. The authors do not thereby assume that the countries and societies so referred to have a necessarily religious character. 'Islamic countries' is used to suggest that these countries and their societies have been *influenced* by Islam. We use these phrases because we do not wish to burden the texts with repeated formulations which may be more precise but also more cumbersome. Most countries in the Middle East are in principle no more 'Islamic' than their European counterparts are 'Christian' inasmuch as their history, tradition and culture have been strongly influenced by Islam or Christianity, but this does not imply that the states themselves are religious.

2   Bassam Tibi, 'Bedroht uns der Islam?', *Der Spiegel*, May 1993, pp. 126–7.

3    The concept of Islamic fundamentalism is very problematic because, as a rule, all manner of differing phenomena which often do not belong together are collected under this heading. Cf. Azmy Bishara's essay in this volume. When we nevertheless use this term here and elsewhere in this book, we do so for lack of any other lexical alternatives. At times, however, we do speak of 'Islamism' or 'political Islam', when we wish to distinguish between different phenomena.

4    Mohamed Sid-Ahmed, 'Muslim World Between Two Fires', *Balkan War Report, Bulletin of the Institute for War and Peace Reporting*, No. 17, January 1993, p.1.

5    K. Armstrong, *Holy War – The Crusades and their Impact on Today's World*, New York: Anchor/Doubleday, 1991.

# 1

# The Perception of Islam in Western Debate

*Andrea Lueg*

'The Sword of Islam', 'The Islamic Threat', 'The Roots of Muslim Rage', 'The Green Peril', 'Islam's New Battlecry': in a veritable flood of publications with these and similar titles, various authors seek to explain 'Islam' to us. Since the Gulf War, the media have discovered the market value of this theme and have been addressing it in television programmes, magazines and books. Meanwhile, the diverse trends and complex social, ethnic or cultural realities in Islamic countries are hardly granted any attention.[1] Islam is seen as a monolithic bloc, and often directly or indirectly equated with Islamic fundamentalism – the 'true Islam'. Simplified and undifferentiated descriptions of Islam in the media fan the flames of vague fears of a supposed threat to Western culture, and create a hostile image of Islam.

For a long time the Islamic Middle East was seen as the polar opposite to the West and as the enemy of Christianity. Even today the region remains alien to the average citizen, making it difficult to place news reports on the area in their proper context. Hardly anything on the Middle East, or on historical clashes or points of contact between the East and West, is learned in schools. Instead of knowledge or at least an unbiased examination of Islamic societies, we have clichés and stereotypes, which apparently make it easier to deal with the phenomenon of Islam. The Western image of Islam is characterised by ideas of aggression and brutality, fanaticism, irrationality, medieval backwardness and antipathy towards women. Although we do have a positive image of 'the Orient' as well, represented by the *Tales of A Thousand and One Nights*, Turkish delight and belly-dancing, this is commonly associated with a more or less bygone fairytale world rather than with Islam. Besides, this view has little or nothing to do with the realities of the Middle East.

Of course the representation of Islam in the Western media is not entirely unanimous. For example, in Germany the same stereotypes are to be found in publications that differ greatly from each other, but in the USA there are significant differences depending on which magazine one reads. Nonetheless, the same patterns come up: these are sometimes superficial, at other times more subtle, and often such portrayals merely show a part of the whole.

'A "selective" presentation and analysis of Islam and events by prominent scholars and political commentators too often inform articles and editorials on the Muslim world', says John Esposito, Director of the Centre for Muslim-Christian Understanding at Georgetown University in Washington. 'This selective analysis fails to tell the whole story ... While it sheds some light, it is a partial light that obscures and distorts the full picture.'[2]

Recently, however, discussion on reporting by the media and political awareness of Islam have developed. Scholars of Islam have recognised that they should not lock themselves away in an ivory tower, leaving the field to popular 'Islam experts'. The media messages, however, hardly change. Instead of serious analyses, they are given to psychologising or to painting crude images of the Islamic world along racist lines.

Certainly, not all elements of the stereotyped fear of the Islamic threat have been invented unaided. In Islamic societies examples of aggression, repression, fanaticism and so on are indeed to be found. But our perception of Islam as 'the enemy' still has little to do with reality, because only certain *aspects* of reality are used to cement our clichéd images. Of course criticising this image-building does not mean accepting all aspects of Islamic societies without criticism. On the contrary: dismantling the image of 'the enemy' is virtually a prerequisite for a constructive critique. This chapter does not set out to explain the 'true Islam', or to change the concept of 'the enemy' into an idealised view. Rather, using concrete examples, I shall examine what mechanisms and methods help to produce this image. What are the elements that are used, and how are they introduced? Perceived threats are built on feelings of fear and insecurity. What are we afraid of in Islam? Are we afraid of the religion or the culture, or is it a concrete physical threat that we perceive? And what is the real point of our image of Islam as hostile? What purpose does it serve in Western societies?

## The 'Islamic Threat'

The Western image of the Islamic world is characterised by terrible news items or apocalyptic visions. Everywhere, one hears of militant Muslims, of 'crazed Islamist zealots', who draw the 'sword of Islam' to assault those of different faiths. There is often talk of an imminent 'religious war', now threatening the former Yugoslavia right in the middle of Europe, because Muslims from all over the world would call on their religious brothers to hurry and help out in the Balkans. 'Soon', writes the German news magazine *Der Spiegel*, 'Europe could have a fanatical theocratic state on its doorstep.'[3] In films we see hordes of Muslims shaking their fists and screaming anti-Western slogans. Muslims are either engaged in fraternal feuds, in Afghanistan for example, or direct their aggression against others, principally the West. Even the American magazine the *New Republic* fears the creeping encroachment of Middle Eastern violence: '[The] bombing [of the World Trade Center in New York] should be occasion to recognize that the violent habits of the Middle East are gradually slipping across our borders.'[4]

Aggression is often made out to be a characteristic of Islam and its followers. In his book *De l'Islam en général et du monde moderne en particulier*, the French author Jean-Claude Barreau writes: 'What could be described as the "great humiliation", and what is indeed present in the basic disposition of the Muslims, can be explained by the origins of their religion: it is warlike, conquest-hungry and full of contempt for the unbeliever.'[5]

Islam as a whole, then, is the aggressor against the West. It embodies 'a theology of conquest and victory, but no theology of defeat'.[6] According to the American news magazine *Time*, 'This is the dark side of Islam, which shows its face in violence and terrorism, intended to overthrow modernizing, more secular regimes and harm the Western nations that support them.'[7] The concept of holy war (jihad), which radical Islamists do indeed use in their call to battle against their adversaries, often crops up in these accounts. Even the secular Saddam Hussein used it in the Gulf War to legitimise his aggressive policies, and many Western commentators were taken in by this pseudo-religious argument. Some Islamic legal scholars supported Saddam while others declared him an apostate and called for jihad against him.[8] The high-ranking Saudi Arabian legal scholar Abdal'aziz ibn Baz described the war by the allies against Iraq as jihad.[9] These contradictions illustrate how easily the concept of jihad can be exploited by people holding widely varying positions and for many different reasons and aims. What the Koran has to say about jihad is, and has been, interpreted in many ways. While some see it as their duty to wage constant war to spread Islam, others believe jihad is intended merely to defend the religion, while still others interpret the idea spiritually as the striving for religious perfection.[10] In the Western media, it is the violent concept of jihad, for which 'Koranic troops' are already whetting their swords in order to avenge themselves for defeats suffered in previous centuries, that is predominant.

Is the West really threatened by a 'holy war' from Muslims 'thirsty for revenge'? Only recently, in the Gulf War, the West demonstrated its staggering military superiority over a well-armed country, tried and tested in warfare, and shaped by Islam. Or is the threat perhaps more psychological or religious, something to do with an alien culture? Islamic religious and cultural symbols can indeed bring emotions to a head, as the 'headscarf affair' in France has shown. Here, some Muslim girls were suspended from school for wearing headscarves and refusing to take them off. The headmaster explained that 'their insistence on wearing headscarves was "provocative and militant".'[11] He would hardly have come out with such a statement in the case of a Christian symbol, such as a cross on a chain. Yet the wearing of headscarves is automatically seen as an attack on Western culture. Only after a long battle did France's highest Administrative Court grant the three girls the right to wear their headscarves.

In his 'threat assessment', Jürgen Liminski explains: 'Non-military elements also come into this analysis. In considering a possible danger to Europe from Islamic areas, they are of special significance.' He is talking about cultural and social aspects here, 'for the use of force ... is ... only one amongst other means of accomplishing the aim of conquest or the desire to rule others.'[12] According to the *New Republic* it is immigrants of Arab origin who pose this threat. '[One] cannot deny that there is also an Arab culture in Brooklyn and Jersey City and Detroit off which the criminals feed and which gets a grim thrill from them. Ours is not a country with which they identify or whose values they share.'[13]

So apparently we are also threatened by a 'holy war' of cultural infiltration and conquest by Islam, whose 'foreignness' is stressed time and again by the Western media. By linking concepts such as aggression, holy war, the aim of conquest, danger and so on with Islam, a sense of threat emerges on three levels: the psychological, the cultural and the religious. But no mention is made of anything which might facilitate access to Islamic culture. At the same time, the 'experts' and the media repeatedly tell us that we have become 'inescapably linked' to this alien culture. The Muslims in the Balkans are Europeans themselves, those in the Maghreb are very close to Europe, and as immigrants in Europe and America they are here among us. This does not, however, make understanding and communication any easier, but increases the feeling of being threatened. So-called experts rule out communication from the outset, and instead stress the 'irreconcilable differences' between the West and Islamic countries. An article in the magazine *Foreign Affairs* by the Harvard professor Samuel Huntington entitled 'The Clash of Civilisations?' attracted much attention not only in America.[14] Here, Huntington explains that future world politics will be determined by conflicts between different civilisations/cultures. According to Huntington, a 'Confucian-Islamic connection' threatening Western interests, values and power is the most important adversary of the West. For Huntington, cultural difference is not one possible factor among others which might contribute to conflicts: it *is* the potential conflict. In saying this he ignores any constructive exchange, any cross-pollination between different cultures, as well as the fact that many values and ideals are shared by different cultures and civilisations. Instead, he stresses threatening differences and unbridgeable rifts, constructs a battle between irreconcilable cultures and falls into the (not so novel) pattern of a culturally defined racism, which has once again become acceptable in the most varying political and social circles.

Although his thesis is simplistic and his arguments are hardly original, with his scenario of cultural battle Huntington has apparently succeeded in catering to commonly felt fears. Many feel their 'hunches' and 'feelings' about foreign cultures are being borne out.

For some, the cultural rift is meanwhile running right through Europe, for '[a] cultural curtain is descending in Bosnia to replace the Berlin Wall, a curtain separating the Christian and Islamic worlds.'[15] Constant reference to unbridgeable rifts that are supposedly yawning between the cultures, and to an image of Islam characterised by aggressive violence turns the foreign culture into something with which there can be no exchange or discussion. On the one hand, the rift is too deep, and on the other hand it is also dangerous. There is no attempt at a dialogue with people from Islamic countries – it might destroy our perception of the Islamic threat or at least render it questionable.

## Islam Equals Fundamentalism

Many people in the West no longer feel connected to Christianity as a religion, but rather as a cultural influence. Their culture is directly or indirectly shaped by it and they do not feel there is anything unusual in this. But, Islam is hardly ever seen as a cultural category, but as a *religion*, one which is threatening. This is particularly so where 'fundamentalism' is concerned, a concept signifying for many a return to the Middle Ages. It is at the same time associated with a pronounced desire for expansion and conquest, coupled with a 'hatred of everything Western'. 'Religious war' is the caption of a photograph in *Time Magazine* showing praying Muslims with their weapons: it continues 'Guns and prayer go together in the fundamentalist battle'.[16]

Fundamentalism is a world-wide phenomenon that is also found outside Islam, in other religions such as Christianity and Judaism. Nonetheless, in the media the term is almost exclusively linked to Islam or even equated with it. Even the renowned British magazine *The Economist* says 'Yet, in a sense, Islam is per se fundamentalist ... In Islam Mosque and State are not to be separated.'[17] Originally, fundamentalism arose in the USA and Great Britain as a protestant counter-movement to the Enlightenment and to modernisation in the middle of the nineteenth century. Its supporters saw themselves as being overrun by social developments such as the consequences of the American Civil War, industrialisation and modernisation. As a result of the Enlightenment, the words of the Bible were subordinated to the rules of reason; a critical interpretation of the Bible had developed. The fundamentalists set their own interpretation against this, according to which the Holy Scriptures were infallibly true in their literal meaning.[18] Our notion of Islamic fundamentalism often leans on this Western concept of fundamentalism which was, however, shaped by our own historical experiences and is therefore not easily transferable to the Islamic world with its different economic and cultural framework.[19]

In the Middle East, there are a number of very different Islamic movements encompassing a spectrum from traditionalist to modernist. In addition, there are groups striving towards secular models of the state, and also non-Muslim minorities such as the approximately 14 million indigenous Christians in the Middle East.[20] Nevertheless, democratic or even pacifist groups from Islamic countries hardly feature in the Western view. To what extent democratic conditions prevail in Islamic countries has mostly been of precious little concern to the West. Dictators such as Saddam Hussein or Hafez Assad were, and in some cases still are, generously supported and armed by the West and the former Soviet Union. Movements wanting to democratise their societies are hardly mentioned in the Western media.

Hostility towards progress, reactionary political ideas and a desire to 'return to the Middle Ages' are all attributed to Islamic fundamentalism. Such patterns are often simply transferred to Islam as a whole. The concept of a 'revolt against modernity' took shape in the media, thereby creating a polarisation between Western modernity and Islamic antiquatedness.[21] 'Does the end of the conflict between the Eastern Bloc and the West, and the rise of unpredictable theocratic states on the edge of Europe, threaten us with ... a new religious war?' asks *Der Spiegel* in obvious allusion to the medieval Crusades.

Elsewhere, it says, 'particularly in the Middle East, the cradle and cultural centre of Islam, bearded extremists are increasingly shaping the image of a militant Islam which is determined by 'Holy War' and blood sacrifice, fanaticism and violence, intolerance and the oppression of women.'[22] By mixing and equating terms such as Muslim, Islamic, fundamentalist and fanatic, everything is ascribed to Islam in general that is at the most applicable to so-called fundamentalism.

For Jean-Claude Barreau, writing on Islam's battle (Islam mind you, not Islamic fundamentalism) against the modern world, in his book *De l'Islam en général*, 'all religions that reject modernity' are either in danger of going under, 'or they embark on a course of bloody opposition to the modern world, and produce fanatics and fundamentalists. Unfortunately, the current relations between Islam and the West appear to be characterised by this second possibility.'[23] Here then, Islam is a religion which rejects modernity and produces fanatics and fundamentalists. This assumes an inevitability that does not exist. Although the phenomena of fanaticism and fundamentalism do exist in Islamic countries, just as they exist in other regions, they are by no means bound to religions, nor are they an inevitable result of religion.

Many authors use the fundamentalists' pattern of argument in their writings on Islam, not crediting Islam with any historical process of development, and instead defining it on the basis of its earliest history or exclusively through the Koran or the tradition of the Prophet. The 'true identity' of Islam, they say (entirely following the fundamentalist argument), lies in the primeval time of the Muslims; alongside the stereotype which arises from this point of view, the complexity of past and current Islamic history is of no consequence. 'This sort of normative definition', says the professor of Islamic studies Reinhard Schulze, 'has clearly fundamentalist features: the dogmatic self-definition of early Islam is seen as the essence of Islam, as the basis of any possibilities of development.'[24] The historical processes that have run through Islam since its early days and have influenced and changed it remain unconsidered, thereby creating the impression that practically no historical change has taken place in the region. Often, it is simply left to the fundamentalists to explain Islam. The Austrian cardinal Franz König, for example, quotes Ayatollah Khomeini of all people in order to prove (using an 'authoritative source') the allegedly inseparable connection between politics and religion in Islam.[25] In this way, fundamentalist positions are transformed into Islamic ones.

The habit of constantly referring today's *social and political* events back to the time of origin of *a religion* ostensibly makes an analysis of the present situation superfluous. Of course there is no denying that religious aspects do play a role in Islamic societies, but the significance of religion must be examined and not simply assumed to be the only pattern of explanation.

In the last few years, the significance of religion has clearly grown in Islamic as in other cultures. What, however, are the specific reasons for this? The attempt to integrate the economy of Islamic countries into the world economy has affected societies in this region as it has every individual. Attributes of 'Westernisation' are to be found in every country and town: scores of Western products drive indigenous products from the market, many school and university teachers have been educated abroad, television brings images of Western culture and Western standards of living into the most remote areas. For many people this has created the desire to defend and protect their own cultural identity against all-powerful Western influences. They see the possibility of doing this by increasingly turning to Islam, which is an expression of their own culture and is not, after all, Western.

With the exception of the 'oil states', Islamic countries have as yet been unable to reach the high standards of living that prevail in the USA and Europe. They belong to the so-called Third World. The sometimes catastrophic economic and social conditions – partly determined by the West – in which people there must live are another reason for the enormous success of Islamist groups. In addition, there are unresolved political problems which have been smouldering for years, such as Palestine.

Neither the adoption of Western models, nor Arab nationalism, nor Marxist models have shown them a way out of their plight. Their representatives have all failed. This situation leaves little room for ideological alternatives. The advantages of Islam as a new hegemonic ideology lie in its ability to transcend borders and establish a Middle Eastern identity, and in the possibility of dissociating oneself from the West and having something to set against it. Islam is deeply rooted in the region as a traditional and culturally significant entity on the one hand, and as the popular religion on the other. For many, it is a value which helps them to orientate themselves in their search for perspectives. This is not true only for Islamists, some of whom try to exploit these facts to achieve their own aims. 'I believe that Islam makes it possible for me to reflect on the big questions of life', explains the Moroccan sociologist Fatima Mernissi for example. 'Yes, this is what I think, and I'm even proud of it. If you now believe that I am a fundamentalist, then so be it. But I think we must protect our cultural legacy from being completely swallowed up by the West.'[26]

It would hardly occur to anyone to describe the committed feminist Fatima Mernissi as a fundamentalist.

The most important reason for the rise in Islamist tendencies could lie in the bankruptcy of all alternative secular ideologies. Radical Islamist groups see the West as the antithesis to their own culture, and categorically reject the Enlightenment, secularisation and the Reformation as values conceived by the 'West'. In so doing they are not directing their activities primarily against the West or Christian Europe, as is often suggested in the media, but are striving towards changing their own societies.

Even the traditional left, and other democratically orientated groups which are open-minded about the West, refer to their own Islamic *culture*. These movements feel they have been left in the lurch by the Western public, which is not concerned with their issues, aims and demands, but merely sees their affiliation to Islam. In reaction to this, such movements have increasingly called for distancing from the West, and for stronger ties to their Islamic identity. In this way our shortsightedness achieves exactly what it fears: the continued encouragement of Islamist tendencies and their radicalisation.

## Oriental Irrationality and the 'Fanatical Masses'

The population explosion in the countries of the Middle East, which is 'spilling over' into Europe and the USA through refugee movements and migration, and which might threaten Western affluence and culture, is an important aspect of the fear of an 'Islamic threat'. This is evident in the constant references to the Arab or Islamic 'masses' by the media. By contrast, there is seldom mention of European, American or even Christian masses. There are very few photographs published of single Muslims.

For Jürgen Liminski, the 'Fundamentalist movement ... is borne by demography. In Iran, half of the roughly 50 million people are younger than 15, in Turkey the population has more than doubled from 20 to 50 million since 1950. In Algeria there are a good 25 million people, where in 1962 there were hardly 10 million. In Egypt, the population has more than tripled in the last fifty years. The pressure from North Africa on Southern Europe is increasing.'[27]

The combined effect of 'Islamic fundamentalism' and the 'masses' increases the element of fear in the media. The rapidly growing Islamic populations are apparently increasing the pressure on European countries. The 'masses' are heading for us, some are already among us as *Gastarbeiter*, immigrant workers. They bring with them their foreign 'hostile' culture and 'fundamentalism', whatever that might mean. In this respect the 'Islamic threat' corresponds with the 'threat from the Third World', because its floods of immigrants and asylum-seekers threaten fortress Europe's affluence. I shall come back to this point in greater detail later.

For the West, there is another aspect to the image of the 'masses' apart from that of threat. It makes distancing possible, so that we do not have to concern ourselves with the individual. The 'masses' are not someone but a threatening something; and this impression is sharpened by connecting it to the image of the 'zealot' and the 'fanatic'. Three out of four French people questioned thought that the word 'fanatical' best applied to Islam.[28] 'Unpredictable passions' seethe in the 'fanatical masses'. For us, fanaticism is a particularly negative and in certain circumstances even dangerous quality with a pathological ring to it, that could easily turn into madness – the exact opposite, then, to the way we like to see ourselves: as sober and rational.

A fanatic or zealot cannot think clearly or act rationally. For many authors, irrationality is an almost essential quality of Muslims. In the German tabloid *Bild Zeitung* Saddam Hussein became the 'madman' during the Gulf War. But even many experts impute a strange way of thinking to Muslims or Arabs (these words are often implicitly equated). 'Conspiracy theories aren't unusual in the Arab world ... I have repeatedly found myself sitting in living rooms and book-lined offices, listening to scholars, businessmen or politicians weave surreal scenarios', explains Ethan Bronner under the revealing headline 'Psycho-Semitic.'[29] Even the former US ambassador to the UN, Jeane Kirkpatrick, questions the ability of Arabs to reach rational decisions: 'The Arab world is the only part of the world where I've been shaken in my conviction that if you let the people decide, they will make fundamentally rational decisions.'[30] The political scientist Bassam Tibi makes it sound as if the people of the Middle East were addicted to oppression.

> The Arab masses follow their dictators and despots till they are bitterly disappointed; they must first undergo painful periods of self-deception before they finally do realise that they have been deceived. However, they do not learn their lesson; though they let their heroes fall, they again pledge allegiance to the next dictator. This is a characteristic of the political culture of the Middle East.[31]

This image of masochistic Arab masses who refuse to learn is not only simplistic, it is also entirely false. Just as in the West, people in the Middle East have no desire to be oppressed.

The stereotype of a supposed irrationality in Islamic countries sharpens the polarisation between East and West. The modern West is sensible, the backward East more or less crazy. As a result it is necessarily impossible for the East to be an equal and valid interlocutor. Madmen are unpredictable and dangerous, one cannot have an equal relationship with them, it is better to keep oneself – or them – at a distance.

## Women and Islam

The harem, the veil and the Turkish cleaning lady with a headscarf are the clichéd images that the West associates with women and Islam. Oriental women appear mostly shrouded in threatening black yards of material – the *chador* – for us the anti-woman medium of repression *par excellence*. The 'head-scarf affair' mentioned above soon become a *'chador* war' in the French media.[32] Since the end of the nineteenth century, the veiling of women has been seen in the West as a symbol of the backwardness of the Islamic countries.

> Veiling – to Western eyes, the most visible marker of differentness and inferiority of Islamic societies – became a symbol now of both the oppression of women … and the backwardness of Islam, and it became the open target of colonial attack and the spearhead of the assault on Muslim societies.[33]

To clarify the issue: the forced veiling of women by men in order to uphold patriarchal structures cannot be justified or accepted. Western women find it almost inconceivable that any woman would voluntarily live according to Islamic dress codes. Yet many women in Islamic countries explain that for them the veil is a symbol of respect for women, allowing them to go about in public more or less without being bothered or degraded as an object. It is also a symbol of their own culture and could therefore come to symbolise resistance to an imposed Westernisation. There are Arab feminists 'who both reject the veil as a personal choice but also recognize its empowering and seductive effect on Arab women'.[34] One can argue about these points, but we should be aware of them and not succumb to the veil ourselves by being unable to see independent and thinking individuals behind it.

The fact that veiling varies in size and shape from country to country and within different social strata is hardly taken into consideration (there is a difference in whether women veil themselves entirely, with only eyes and hands remaining uncovered, or wear a headscarf). There is little variation in the image of the Islamic woman offered by the media: she serves man and is oppressed by him, be it (based on past ideas about harems or polygamy) as one among many other wives, or as the cleaning lady in the West who must always walk three steps behind her husband, or even as the woman who lives the spoilt 'life of luxury' in the Arab ruling houses so beloved by the tabloids – she remains passive and dependent. From the gossip column to the feminist magazine, Islamic women are mainly this: victims. As such, they are merely objects of reporting, never allowed to speak for themselves. Women from Islamic countries are sometimes even perceived as a threat because they are victims. They are seen as immigrating to the West from their homelands *en masse*. 'One Western official, who requested anonymity, put it this way: "Consider that there are one billion Muslims in the world, so we're talking hypothetically about 500 million women who might want out."'[35]

Under the title 'A Stick in the Back, a Child in the Belly' *Der Spiegel* described the 'quiet and hidden martyrdom' of Turkish women in Germany, 'whose billowing robes and old-maid scarves' have made them a laughing-stock.[36] 'They are terrorised and beaten, and live in constant fear of their violent husbands, brothers or male relatives who have total power over everyone in the family who wears a dress.' *Der Spiegel* is not interested in the countless young Turkish, Arab and Persian women leading independent lives in the West, or in those whose family life may differ from their German and British equivalents but is still different from life 'in wildest Kurdistan'. 'Women's refuges in Germany', writes *Der Spiegel*, 'are full of Turkish women.' It seems to have escaped *Der Spiegel* that the overwhelming majority of women in such refuges are seeking shelter from the violence of German men. Instead of Turkish women themselves, it is a sociologist from Frankfurt, 'Mrs König, expert on the Turks', who tells us all about the conditions in Turkish families. The title of a special issue of the feminist magazine *EMMA* ('War. The Effects of Male Madness and How Women Offer Resistance') is adorned by the picture of a Muslim woman veiled in black from head to toe, with a blood red crown of thorns placed on her head by a photo montage, the symbol of Jesus, who, according to Christian tradition, sacrificed himself on the cross.

Betty Mahmoody's best-seller *Not Without My Daughter* (which incidentally sold ten times as many copies in Germany as in the USA) drew in its wake a wave of publications on the life of women in Islamic countries or married to Muslims.[37] The more dramatic and brutal the story the better. The women allowed to give their accounts in these publications had to be 'Prisoners in their own country', 'Sold into slavery by their own fathers' or 'Sentenced to death by their own families'.

Islam is most often seen as the main reason for the oppression of Middle Eastern women, even though we have learned that as far as veiling and polygamy are concerned, the latter generally the exception rather than the rule, the Koran allows for various interpretations.[38] Female circumcision is also no invention of Islam, but was already practised in Pharaonic Egypt, although this does not make it any less objectionable.

There is no research on possible non-religious reasons for the situation of women in Islam or even on the possible exploitation of religion. Industrial underdevelopment, for example, is a big problem for many Islamic countries, leading to a bad economic situation with an over-stretched labour market, which in turn negatively affects the professional possibilities for women. Similarly to Western countries, Arab countries also try to create a 'reserve workforce' of women who remain at the disposal of the labour market and can be sent back to the kitchen stove when they are not needed. A glance at the statistics of Western countries is enough to establish that even here it is the women who are the first to disappear from the labour market in economically precarious situations. The high birth rates in Islamic countries hinder access to working life for many women. Finally, women there live within a patriarchal value system which is strongly orientated towards the family, although this does not have its roots mainly or only in religion. In most Middle Eastern countries, the Sharia (Islamic law) is valid, at least formally, and is exploited to some extent by governments or radical Islamic groups to prevent women from achieving an equal position in society. The Sharia, however, lends itself to widely varying interpretations, as the Tunisian example shows: it is the only Arab country which allows abortion under certain circumstances, a position based on the expert opinion of an Islamic legal scholar, a *fatwa*.[39]

This begs the question why connections between the situation of women in Islamic countries and the prevailing economic and patriarchal systems there – connections which also play a role in Western societies – are hardly mentioned in the press, while Islam is placed centre-stage as women's number one enemy.

'As I see it, it is often the Western point of view and not so much Islam that ascribes the role of victim to women in Islamic countries', says Martina Sabra.[40] Indeed while travelling through Islamic countries one does come across many women who simply do not play the role of victim, and who do not see themselves in this light at all. Clearly, the cliché of the oppressed Islamic woman serves the purpose of distracting us from things that are wrong in our own society. These defects appear more acceptable if someone else's experience is even worse. As far as Islam as the 'enemy' is concerned, the problem of women's oppression can be pushed far aside, on to other equally 'Islamic countries', which differ from our 'secular states'. Such a point of view allows us to look down on the Islamic countries and reassure ourselves about our own superiority. 'In the mass media, the stylisation of the "oppressed woman behind the veil" [functions] as a symbol of the "medieval backwardness" of Islamic states, and provides fodder for the outlined discourse on the superiority of the West', writes Anne-Kathrin Reulecke.[41] In no way can we deny that religious ideology is a contributing factor to the oppression of women in the Middle East. Christianity has played a similarly negative role in the West but in both Christian cultural areas and in Islamic countries, this religious factor is only one of many and not necessarily the most important.

I am by no means concerned with defending 'Islam' or abandoning criticism of the mechanisms of oppression against women. I do consider it important, however, to present the far more complex picture of conditions in Islamic countries, and the reasons for the repression and oppression of women. Moreover, Islamic women should speak for themselves, and we should accept them as individuals. We will not be doing the situation justice as long as we continue to take cover behind the cliché of the Islamic woman as victim. We must *analyse* discrimination against women by taking into account the real social conditions, as we do for women in the West, instead of assuming we 'know' in advance that this is due to mainly religious reasons. A more equal dialogue could be achieved in this way.

## The Superiority of the West

The Western notion of 'the enemy' is about clearly marking out the divisions and creating a scheme which distinguishes friend from foe. First of all this means that the enemy must be *different* from us. 'Most Islamic countries in the Middle East live according to a world of associations which cannot be judged by European standards, a world of of bazaars, mosques and the apparatus of repression', writes Jürgen

Liminski.[42] He paints a picture of a structure that is difficult to see through and thus hides Western insecurity. According to this scheme, the West is progressive, rational, enlightened and secular. Islam is backward, fanatical, irrational and fundamentalist. What is interesting is that it is not Islam and Christianity that are contrasted, or the West and the East, but Islam and the West, a religion and a geographical area. Furthermore, it is clearly very important for us in the West to feel superior and to see Western culture as the 'best' and 'most progressive'.

'The Islamic militants do not understand what is going on', says Jean-Claude Barreau. 'They do not realise that they have been beaten by a modernity whose rationality is superior to the Muslim one.' The rationally superior modernity is not only the West that overcame the Orient, in the person of Napoleon in Egypt in July 1798 (which is what the quote refers to), but the West that has been doing so ever since. According to Barreau, this is how it will be in the future: 'They can buy modern weapons and even deploy them, but the victories of the West are not dependent on the quality of weapons alone, but rather on the "system" of its organisation.'[43] In the Gulf War, Western dominance was demonstrated in its ability to kill more efficiently. At the same time, it was possible to justify the military action and the many victims of this war more easily by using an image of people in Islamic countries as inferior to us and therefore of less value. 'We caught them with their pants down. They were still in their sleeping bags. It was just like shooting turkeys' was how the American company commander Jess Fairington expressed himself after a helicopter gunship attack on Iraqi positions during the Gulf War.[44] The war seen as turkey shooting, people as turkeys – does this illustrate the civilising superiority of the West? Only if we measure civilising superiority in terms of standards of weapons technology.

The Enlightenment and the related separation of religion and state count among the most important aspects of Western superiority. In our eyes whoever fails to fulfil this separation is immature and bound by religion. We believe we have displaced religion from the public arena into the private one, and have thereby somehow overcome it. Islam nonetheless terrifies us *as a religion* – and it is precisely through this religious element, to which we restrict our perception, that the rift between the Orient and the Occident is made even deeper.

Anything we hear from the Islamic world, we assume to be stated from an inferior position, and in a religious context, i.e. that of Islam. We do not try to understand Islam as a religion, but instead often reject it on principle. I am not defending Islam or any other faith, but one cannot help noticing what terror a religion manages to spread in a supposedly secular society. The reactions to Islamic movements are anything but rational and enlightened. Yet much of the Western media set much store by factual and objective reporting. Islamic countries have clearly not been through a period of enlightenment in the Western sense. But must they adhere rigidly to the Western pattern, can they not find their own way to enlightenment, freedom and democracy? The theory of the 'unity of religion and state' as an intrinsic characteristic of Islam, often seen as a truism, is a well-loved prejudice which does not improve with constant repetition (see Chapter 5 by Azmy Bishara). In fact most countries of the Middle East today have more or less secular governments, such as those of Egypt, Tunisia or Turkey.

Human rights, which received world-wide recognition through the United Nations Universal Declaration of Human Rights, are often cited as a 'Western product' and another symbol of Occidental superiority. Islam, by contrast, is portrayed as being hostile to human rights, as an ideological structure which is virtually antithetical to the Western understanding of human rights. 'Freedom of thought', according to *Der Spiegel*, 'is, like every other human right, un-Islamic.'[15] They might as well say: 'there are no human rights in Islam.'

What this overlooks is that Islam is not a unified and contained whole. Within Islamic societies there are interesting debates on Western patterns of thinking and living, as well as on the question of human rights. Moreover, there are even attempts to put forward an Islamic concept of human rights and a universal Islamic declaration of human rights.

The *actual situation* of human rights and democracy in most Islamic countries is certainly shocking. In many of these countries torture is commonplace, and press censorship, the death penalty and, above all, unequal treatment of men and women are to be found everywhere. These are all totally unacceptable conditions, which must be denounced constantly until the conditions of the people improve.

Yet we must nonetheless ask who or what is responsible for these catastrophic conditions. The Western media again often make Islam out to be the main evil, and they love to divert our attention to the belief of 'Islamic zealots', namely that 'human rights are an imported Western body of thought' and are therefore to be rejected. This position is certainly widespread but by no means predominant. Besides, we should not forget that even in the Western Christian cultural area human rights are often trampled underfoot and openly abused. Latin American and even European history have many such examples. The abuse of human rights can be more closely related to the intensity of social conflicts and to the political instability of the corresponding forms of government than to religion.

The supposed inferiority of Islamic countries is repeatedly explained by the fact that followers of Islam are 'bound' by their faith which forswears or prevents every process of modernisation. In Islamic countries, there is and has been a position of radical denial whose representatives reject such concepts as freedom, enlightenment, human rights and democracy because they come from the West. Analysis and reporting on and of such groups should certainly not be neglected. 'But they do not rule the Islamic camp either intellectually or quantitatively. It is not denial that dominates here, but rather a critical discussion of one's own traditions and Western patterns of thinking and living.'[46] A more detailed portrayal of such views would of course disturb the image of the superior West. There are only few attempts at an open and critical dialogue with representatives from Islamic countries on the issues of enlightenment, human rights, the relationship between religion and the state, or the supposed Western values which come under criticism in Western societies as well. Instead, the solutions which the West believes it has found for its specific problems are considered to be universally valid. Whoever does not accept them must surely be backward or irrational; conversely, whatever is not antiquated in Islamic countries must necessarily come from the West.

Cultural development is often measured by comparison with Western culture. With this ethnocentric stance, the West only betrays those opposed to the oppression and terror legitimised as 'Islamic' in the Middle East. 'The existential threat posed by radical fundamentalist Muslims and the fear of being misused for Eurocentric interests', writes Arzu Toker, has 'paralysed many critical Muslims.'[47]

### Why This Hostile Image?

The need constantly to emphasise the dominance of Western countries and Western culture over Islamic countries is apparently of particular concern to the Western public. Exactly what need does this hostile image fulfil in our societies?

Examples of misogyny, aggression, fanaticism and irrationality are to be found in the West, as they are in Islamic countries. The racist attacks and riots throughout Europe in the early 1990s serve as a reminder of what slumbers beneath the gloss of our own civilisation. In Europe, and particularly in the USA, more and more people are turning to religion and even to 'fundamentalism'. However, we apparently do not look upon such occurrences as a part of or an expression of our culture, but as unrelated and external to it. Even National Socialism, fascism and Stalinism are considered by many to be historical 'accidents' and are not associated with Christian Western culture. We use completely different standards when we confront the same or different phenomena in other cultures, especially Islamic ones.

> Many failed to make the same distinctions with regard to Islam and Islamic organizations between the actions of a radical minority and the mainstream majority that were made so easily when ... the world watched the Branch Davidian sect, an extremist 'Christian' group in Waco, Texas, kill FBI agents and, protected by an astonishing arsenal of weapons, hold off federal authorities for weeks.[48]

A certain lack of knowledge helps when we talk about Islam. There is a noticeable discrepancy between our knowledge of 'Islam' on the one hand and the certainty of our judgements on the other. 'I don't know anything about Islam, but', is certainly one of the most common phrases to be heard in discussions on the subject. And nobody wants to be shaken out of this 'I don't know', for it allows us to construct another world, the Islamic world, even though our construction does not correspond with the reality of Islamic countries. We invent an Islam that suits us, that best fulfils our politico-psychological needs. This is exactly how we arrive at a clean separation between 'us' and 'them' (the Other), between inside and outside that are never supposed to meet and we thus succeed in fencing off and fortifying our own Western identity. Similarities and parallels between the cultures would only disturb this image, because it would mean recognising ourselves in the Other and blur the distinctions. Instead, we stress the differentness of Islamic countries and Islamic culture, and 'the Orient' is stylised as the antithesis to the West. We thus create a polar opposite against which we can assure ourselves of our 'self' and of our values, and against which we can shape our perception of our Western world. This need to reassure ourselves appears to be becoming more and more important, especially in view of the debates on declining values and identity crises that are the order of the day in the West. With the end of the Cold War, the enemy against whom we could all band together has disappeared. 'In the last forty years the industrial countries of the West ... have developed and defined themselves as antipodes to "real Socialism",' according to the political scientist Franz Nuscheler. 'The loss of this identity-giving distinction has led to a search for a replacement. Islam has presented itself as one. Particularly since the Gulf War, which was also interpreted as a war against the West.'[49] At the same time, it serves as a site for projection, a place to which we can banish the negative aspects of our culture. An example is the oppression of women. We cannot deny that this exists in the West too, but the situation is much worse in Islamic countries, so the need to criticise them is the more pressing.

The anti-Islamic image of the enemy is part of a more extensive fear of the Third World. Dangers and threats which are more often of a social, political or cultural nature rather than a military one, also seem to come from the poor South. The Third World as a whole, not just the Islamic Middle East, is seen as a place of instability, insecurity, of tribal and civil wars, incomprehensible violence, disease and countless other evils. These regions of misery and unrest stand in contrast to the apparently well- and clearly-ordered West. The affluence in the West stands out against the reality of need in the developing countries, and is to be psychologically (and if need be materially) defended. The fear of the Third World is in a certain sense a fear of poverty, a fear of being infected again by its evils. This is another reason why migration from Islamic countries is perceived to be so threatening: the Third World is coming to us, forming bridgeheads in our cities. Perhaps these islands will also bring their misery to us?

One of the preconditions of this fear lies in the fact that the West is no longer as sure of its achievements as it would like to be. This does not only apply to the rational, enlightened and secular character of Western societies, which is constantly being called into question by racism, fundamentalist bishops or 'tribal' and religious wars as in former Yugoslavia or Northern Ireland. It is also applicable to the really important civilising value of the West: material wealth. Today, even this is, at least, unsure: even the middle classes could soon face financial ruin.

The Western standard of living – our wealth – is being threatened, and this is another reason why fear of poverty is an important factor. This poverty is represented by the Third World, whose religion, as the West perceives it, is Islam. Other religions such as Hinduism are perhaps culturally and geographically too distant. Fear of Islam is also an ideological-religious version of the fear of the future. This is then associated with and highlighted by truly destabilising, threatening or costly developments, such as environmental catastrophes, large-scale migration and the influx of refugees, as well as by the increase and radicalisation of political or politico-religious movements.

'The newness and unpredictability of such dangers makes many people in industrialised countries feel insecure. Thus people fear 'that "migrating man" could also one day be used as a "weapon"', and 'fear of an invasion by outsiders – Muslim fundamentalists and terrorists, starving Africans, people fleeing from conflicts in the Third World – is spreading in Western Europe.'[50]

The *New Republic* has established: 'There are many aggrieved peoples in the world, and millions of these aspire to become Americans', among them many from Islamic countries. Earlier waves of Arab immigrants were more willing to assimilate,

> making, more or less, a clean break with the old world ... But this cannot be said about many in the last large contingent of Arab immigrants, not a few of them illegals. They were also fleeing from the fires of their world. But the fires were ones that they had helped set. Unlike their predecessors, they carried the wars in their hearts with them.[51]

Islam has long functioned as the antithesis of the West. The cultural conflict between the West and its 'archetypal enemy Islam' clearly lies deeper than that between the West and the Third World as a whole.

> For nearly three hundred years, the Orient has served the self-definition of the modern Occident, that is to say, at first of Europe and then of the West. In the process, the Middle Eastern cultural area acquired a variety of very different 'functions' in the emergence of the Occidental order.[52]

Clichés and stereotypes about Islam have held fast over centuries in our societies, and have been passed on from generation to generation and become deeply rooted. They are potentially to hand, and can be quickly activated when it appears to be politically expedient, as during the Gulf War for example.

When I criticise the emphasis placed on Islamic countries as the Other, it is by no means a denial of the 'otherness' of Islamic culture or Islamic societies in comparison to Western culture. What must be criticised, however, is the unequal portrayal of parallels and differences by the media, and the almost automatically negative evaluation of all that differs from Western culture. We do not meet the Other with a desire to understand. Rather, this Other derives from a comparison which suggests that our own culture is more comprehensible and therefore – usually – better. In the Western press,

Islamic countries are not presented (as we have seen from some examples) as members of a principally equal cultural system. This would demand that we be aware of cultural differences and similarities, and give them consideration, including mutual criticism on the one hand and recognition of similarities, both positive and negative on the other. What is negative in Islamic culture may well exist in the West too. In this way our own values and the image of our own culture could be called into question. But the idealising and positive self-image of the West must on no account be destroyed, and so our stereotyped image of Islam becomes a crutch for our own cultural identity.

The West concentrates on Islam *as a religion* which is made out to be responsible for countless political, cultural and social phenomena in Islamic countries. And it is clearly Islam as a religion that generates such fear in Western culture, a fear of religion that we thought we had banished from our enlightened societies. To quote Reinhard Schulze:

> The West appears to re-enact, indeed to prove its own Enlightenment and its own independence from the power of religion by comparison with the Orient. This is surely also because doubts have arisen about the victory of the world over religion, or of reason over irrationality in the West itself.[53]

The Western fear of religion is projected on to the Islamic world. Perhaps people in the West are entertaining doubts about the achievements of Western civilisation, about rationality and enlightenment, and think they can be better protected by defending themselves against a 'threat' from outside. At least, many in the West do not feel secure and superior enough to confront Islam and Islamic 'fundamentalism' with complete composure or the necessary critical detachment. As a religion Islam fulfils its function of 'a threat'. The supposed *religious* identity of Islamic countries is the exact opposite of European self-definition.

> This focusing of attention on Islam as a religion is, in my opinion, the most disastrous thing the West could do as regards Middle Eastern societies at the moment. It is the greatest and most far-reaching cultural stricture passed by us on Middle Eastern societies, because we no longer maintain that social structures similar and equal to ours can exist in Middle Eastern societies.[54]

What is threatening about Islam often stems from a limited vision rather than from reality.

In the Middle East, our constant fear of the 'Islamic threat' is mirrored in the concept of the 'Christian West' as the enemy, a concept which mainly serves the purposes of right-wing Islamists.

> The protagonists of radical Islam ... may be the last people in the world who still talk about 'the West' as if it were a clearly identifiable place. From Morocco to Indonesia, something called the West is presented as The Other: an opposite that challenges Islam.[55]

The West is accused of aggressiveness, expansionist desires and intolerance. In the West spiritual decadence and declining morals prevail and women are degraded as sex objects. This clichéd image of the West shows remarkable structural similarities to our clichéd image of Islam. For the Middle East, the Occident serves as a site on to which everything considered irreconcilable with its own societies can be projected. The difference lies in the fact that in Islamic countries the West's claim to superiority and real superiority are felt to be threatening. Over the last decades many Muslims have begun to feel a constant obligation to defend their own culture and beliefs against Western accusations which often spring from our simplistic view of Islam. Thus, our hostile perception of Islam is an important factor behind their extremely defensive posture and the creation and reinforcement of a hostile counter-perception of the West. Latent in this interplay is the danger that the two cultures may become less ready for dialogue. In both the Orient and the Occident, this would only strengthen the position of those who see an unbridgeable gulf between East and West.

The reciprocal perceptions of the West and Islam as 'the enemy' were and are ideologically abused. Along with increasing hostility towards foreigners and growing racism in the West, the imagined Islamic threat could in the future be more effectively exploited by internal politics than it has ever been before. It is no coincidence that the Austrian right-wing populist Jörg Haider always serves up the story of parents of Muslim children who allegedly demand that crucifixes be removed from classrooms, adding 'We didn't fight the Turkish wars to see all we secured changed in roundabout ways.'[56] In the future this view of Islam will pose a greater problem for Western societies than the 'Islamic threat' itself.

The political scientist Franz Nuscheler says

I am not as afraid of the new threats being built up there as I am of the reactions in the North, in our own societies. What goes on daily before our eyes as regards policies on asylum seekers and refugees gives me greater reason for fear than Islamic fundamentalism or the growing number of asylum seekers. The image of the South as 'the enemy' does not only strengthen prejudice but also breeds racism and gives wide and effective support to sealing off fortress Europe. It is not Europe's military security, not its affluence that are threatened, it is its humanitarianism.[57]

# Notes

1   See Note 1 of the Introduction.

2   J. L. Esposito, *The Islamic Threat – Myth or Reality?*, New York and Oxford: Oxford University Press, 1992, p. 173.

3   'Unser Marsch hat begonnen', *Der Spiegel*, No. 5, 1993, p. 108.

4   'The Bomb Threat', *New Republic*, 29 March 1993, p. 9.

5   Jean-Claude Barreau, *De l'Islam en général et du monde moderne en particulier*, Paris: Belfont-Le Pré aux Clercs, 1991.

6   ibid.

7   'The Dark Side of Islam', *Time Magazine*, 4 October 1993, p. 62.

8   'Kalif oder Ketzer', *Der Spiegel*, No. 6, 1991, p. 162.

9   See R. Schulze, 'Alte und neue Feindbilder. Das Bild der arabischen Welt und des Islam im Westen', in Georg Stein (ed.), *Nachgedanken zum Golfkrieg*, Heidelberg: Palmyra Publ., 1991, p. 246 (footnotes).

10   'Erbfeinde aus Unverständnis', *Die Zeit*, 20 November 1992.

11   *Die Tageszeitung*, 4 November 1992.

12   J. Liminski, 'Europas Bedrohung durch den islamischen Radikalismus', *Das Parlament*, No. 3/4, 10/17 January 1992.

13   'The Immigrants', *New Republic*, 19 April 1993, p. 7.

14   S. Huntington, 'The Clash of Civilisations?', *Foreign Affairs*, Vol. 72, No. 3, Summer 1993, pp. 22–49.

15   R. D. Kaplan, 'Ground Zero – Macedonia: The Real Battleground', *New Republic*, 2 August 1993, pp. 15–16, here p. 16.

16   'The Dark Side of Islam', *Time Magazine*, 4 October 1993, p. 63.

17   'Islam Resumes its March', *The Economist*, 4 April 1992, p. 63.

18   H. Schäfer, 'Religiöser Fundamentalismus als Ermächtigungsstrategie', *Ökumenische Rundschau*, 41, Vol. 4, October 1992, pp. 434–48.

19   H. Scheer, 'Europa und der islamische "Fundamentalismus"', *Leviathan*, 19, Vol. 1, 1991, pp. 21–31.

20   H. Anschütz, 'Die prekäre Lage des orientalischen Christentums', *Das Parlament*, No. 37–8, 6/13 September 1991.
21   Cf. also T. Meyer, *Fundamentalismus – Aufstand gegen die Moderne*, Reinbek: Rowholt Publ., 1991.
22   'Unser Marsch hat begonnen', *Der Spiegel*, No. 5, 1993, p. 112.
23   Barreau, *De l'Islam en général*.
24   R. Schulze, 'Politischer Islam und westliche Mißverständnisse', *Blätter des iz3w*, No. 172, March/April 1991, p. 20.
25   'It is Ayatollah Khomeini who said: "Without politics Islam is nothing"'. Cardinal Franz König, 'Die Vergangenheit beiseite lassen', *Die Zeit*, No. 49, 27 November 1992.
26   Interview in *Die Tageszeitung*, 15 December 1989.
27   Liminski, 'Europa's Bedrohung'.
28   'Mit Kopftuch in die Schule', *Frankfurter Rundschau*, 7 December 1992.
29   E. Bronner, 'Psycho-Semitic', *New Republic*, 24 May 1993, p. 17.
30   Quote taken from: M. Kramer, 'Islam vs. Democracy', *Commentary*, Vol. 95, No. 1, January 1993, pp. 35–42, here p. 37.
31   B. Tibi, 'Über die Schwierigkeiten der Europäer arabische Politik zu verstehen', in Georg Stein (ed.), *Nachgedanken zum Golfkrieg*, Heidelberg, 1991, pp. 97–107, here pp. 102–3.
32   'Mit Kopftuch in die Schule', *Frankfurter Rundschau*, 7 December 1992.
33   L. Ahmed, *Women and Gender in Islam*, New Haven: Yale University Press, 1993, p. 152.
34   Lama Abu Odeh, 'Post-colonial Feminism and the Veil: Thinking the Difference', *Feminist Review*, No. 43, Spring 1993, p. 26.
35   A. L. Bardach, 'Tearing off the Veil', *Vanity Fair*, August 1993.
36   *Der Spiegel*, No. 44, 1990, p. 99.
37   Anne-Kathrin Reulecke, 'Die Befreiung aus dem Serail', *Feministische Studien*, 9. Jahrgang 2, November 1991, pp. 8–20; Betty Mahmoody, *Not Without My Daughter*, New York: St Martin's Press, 1993.
38   F. Mernissi, *Der politische Harem – Mohammed und die Frauen*, Frankfurt: Herder Publ., 1989.
39   M. Sabra, 'Frauenrecht – Menschenrecht', *Blätter des iz3w*, No. 172, March/April 1991, pp. 26–9.
40   ibid.
41   Reulecke, 'Die Befreiung'.
42   Liminski, 'Europa's Bedrohung'.
43   Barreau, *De l'Islam en général*.
44   *Die Zeit*, No.10, 1 March 1991, p. 2.
45   'Wasserstoffbombe des Islam', *Der Spiegel*, No. 8, 1991, p. 149.

46  G. Krämer, 'Kritik und Selbstkritik: Reformistisches Denken im Islam', in Michael Lüders (ed.), *Der Islam im Aufbruch? – Perspektiven der arabischen Welt*, Munich: Piper Publ., 1992, p. 212.

47  A. Toker, 'Eurozentrisches Feindbild oder Kritik am Islam?', *beiträge zur feministischen theorie und praxis*, 35, 1993, pp. 115–22, here p. 116.

48  Esposito, *The Islamic Threat*, p. ix.

49  Prof. F. Nuscheler, University of Duisburg, lecture in Cologne, September 1991.

50  V. Matthies, 'Neues Feindbild Dritte Welt: Verschärft sich der Nord-Süd Konflikt?', *Aus Politik und Zeitgeschichte*, Vol. 25–6, 14 June 1991, pp. 3–11, here p. 5.

51  'The Immigrants', *New Republic*, 19 April 1993.

52  R. Schulze, 'Weil sie ganz anders sind – Alte Klischees verstellen uns den Blick auf einen Orient im Aufbruch', *Die Zeit*, No. 10, 1 March 1991.

53  R. Schulze, 'Islam und Herrschaft. Zur politischen Instrumentalisierung einer Religion', in M. Lüders (ed.), *Der Islam im Aufbruch? – Perspektiven der arabischen Welt*, Munich, 1992, pp. 94–129, here p. 102.

54  R. Schulze, lecture in Cologne, September 1991.

55  'Everything the Other is not', *The Economist*, 1 August 1992.

56  'Österreich oder Anständigkeit zuerst?', *Frankfurter Rundschau*, 29 January 1993.

57  Nuscheler, lecture in Cologne, September 1991.

# 2

# From Romanticisation to Colonial Dominance: Historical Changes in the European Perception of the Middle East

*Petra Kappert*

'Europe and the Orient' was the title of a spectacular exhibition in the Berlin Gropius Bau in 1989. Here, a monumental display of artefacts bore witness to the Orient's 1,100-year-old power over the imagination of the West.

This chapter will discuss the influence of the Orient on the Occident and, to a lesser extent vice versa. It is still relevant today to examine this close, albeit ambivalent relationship, for as a result of the second Gulf War and the collapse of communism in Europe, the West is looking for and moulding new concepts of 'the enemy', which it may already have found in Islamic fundamentalism.

I shall confine myself to what I consider to be three important aspects which are not, however, equally well known. The first concerns the European construct of the *imaginary* Orient as a fantasised 'counter-world', which poets and Orientalists, principally in the nineteenth century, dreamed up and set against their own Western reality. The second, less well-known aspect will show how concepts central to European thought, such as *freedom*, were carefully adapted against great resistance; the example used is the reception of the ideas of the French Revolution in the Ottoman empire and Egypt – the two countries of the Islamic East that first showed signs of 'Westernisation'. The final aspect concerns how enthusiasm for the 'Oriental dreamworld' gave way to a desire actually to be there – as a disciplinarian, of course – particularly among Germany at the turn of the century.

'There is no Orient', the Orientalist and expert on Islam Maxime Rodinson once said.[1] One could add, there is not the Orient regarded by today's academics as having represented a unity of peoples, countries, regions, societies and cultures with common (permanent or temporary) features. In the course of the historical development of the relationship 'between the East and the West', the image of the

Orient from the point of view of the Occident was subject to a number of changes in substance and emphasis, and this is still the case today. Since the Mediterranean Orient has been decisively shaped by religion both culturally and politically since the eighth century, *Islam* is the unifying and determining element underlying the European evaluation of the region as a 'unified whole'.

Between the tenth and fourteenth centuries, the Islamic world had a lasting influence on Western Europe. With the help of Middle Eastern Christian and Jewish translators and scholars the knowledge of the ancients was handed down and developed. Europe participated in this process and eventually, by building on it, laid the foundations of the modern natural sciences and humanities. The knowledge of the ancients that had been safeguarded in the Arabic world made its way to Europe between the tenth and thirteenth centuries through Syrian, Arabic and Jewish translators and commentators.[2] Reports of the legendary wealth of the Orient can also be found in texts from the Christian Middle Ages.

Since the fifteenth century, the importance of the Islamic world for Europe has been characterised less by direct cultural influence than by the awareness of a political and military threat. With the decline of the Byzantine empire and the establishment of Ottoman rule on its ruins in former Constantinople in 1453, and then the Ottoman expansion in the Balkans up to the gates of Vienna, the Orient presented Europe with a principally 'Turkish face'. This, according to Luther, bore the features of the apocalyptic Antichrist and spread terror, barbarity and a new religion 'with fire and sword'. A flood of tracts and leaflets bear witness to the fear of the Turks and to this image of the Turkish enemy till late into the seventeenth century, especially in German-speaking Central Europe.[3]

Of all the countries of the Middle East, Turkey had, over the centuries, developed the closest political, military and economic ties with the West. In the sixteenth century, after conquering Arabia and North Africa (Syria, Palestine, Egypt, Tunisia and Algeria) the Ottomans had achieved supremacy in the Mediterranean and left the stamp of their rule on the entire region. (From 1517 the Sultan in Istanbul laid claim to the title of caliph, i.e. the title of the spiritual leader of all Sunni Muslims.)

## The Orient as Dreamworld

The transformation of the Orient into a romantic dreamworld could only come about in Europe after the defeat of the second Turkish siege of Vienna (1683) and the continual repulse of Ottoman rule in the seventeenth and eighteenth centuries. Then the once powerful enemy began to lose its terror. In the Western imagination of the eighteenth-century age of Enlightenment, the dark and sinister image of the threatening Orient of the Middle Ages gradually began to brighten and change to some extent.

'Tout est galant, traitable et gracieux' is how a 1750 ballad by La Fontaine describes the convivial nature of life in the far Ottoman empire, a life he considered characterised by easy living, luxury and fairytale displays of splendour, boundless pleasure, blue skies and a mild climate – the Orient as a distant, bucolic, rococo province.[4]

Between 1704 and 1717, the French Orientalist Jean-Antoine Galland published his translation of *Tales from a Thousand and One Nights*. This view of Oriental life, which also stole a glance behind the locked doors of mysterious women's chambers, was henceforth to fire the imagination of those in the royal courts of Europe and the salons of the educated. However, as Rodinson puts it, the notion of the 'equality of the natural endowment of all peoples', which was being spread through the 'active optimism of the true religion of the Enlightenment', led to a partial revision of reservations about a 'barbaric' Islamic world, as it had been defined in the Middle Ages.[5] For many eighteenth-century Europeans, the Muslims were people whose customs and traditions were worth discovering and who could quite well be 'morally' equal to the Christians.

At the same time, however, representatives of the Enlightenment evoked another picture: that of Oriental *despotism*. From now on, this image was to endure in Western minds alongside the illusion of the exotic fairytale Islamic world. Montesquieu and Voltaire criticised the Orient as the place of anti-Enlightenment, ruled by cruel despots exercising unrestrained violence over their subjects. This, of course, allowed the image of the self-changing Occident to shine all the more brightly. In this definition, the concept of Oriental despotism takes on the features of a 'strange and exotic *Masculine Genre*', an appraisal that was to undergo fundamental change in nineteenth-century Europe.[6]

From his youth, Johann Wolfgang von Goethe had also felt drawn to the simultaneous strangeness and closeness of Islamic culture (at 23 he had drafted a tragedy on the life of the Prophet Muhammad). His interest, however, focused mainly on the question of the nature of Oriental poetry and on the conditions under which it was able to develop.[7] In 1814 he acquainted himself with the complete works of the medieval Persian poet, Hafiz (who died in 1389) in J. von Hammer-Purgstall's translation and took it as a model for his own creation: in 1819 Goethe's *West-Östlicher Divan* appeared with a prose section entitled *Noten und Abhandlungen*, on which he addressed the public with his studies on Oriental poetry. How greatly the multi-faceted personality of the poet Hafiz interested him has been stressed time and again. Apart from this, however, it is Goethe's image of the Orient that presents us with yet another aspect of the way Europeans saw the Islamic world in the early nineteenth century: in Goethe's eyes, the Orient was 'a fresh and simple region', of which the long-forgotten world of the 'natural' Bedouin served as the most striking example.[8] He admired the 'moral principles' represented by 'firm devotion to members of the tribe, desire for honour, courage, the irreconcilable desire for revenge moderated by the pain of love, charity, sacrifice, all boundless'. The demands of the Prophet Muhammad (whom he also admired as a poet) gained his admiration on closer study; for they were entirely appropriate to the practical needs of a nation.[9] By contrast, he felt his contemporary Europe to be 'educated, over-educated, miseducated and over-complicated'. To him Europe seemed 'too dry, ordered and prosaic'.[10]

Even his evaluation of *despotism* in the Orient does not give as black an impression as that of many eighteenth-century authors. Above all, he recognised its advantages for the poet: 'In the royal courts and in the company of the Great, a view of the world is opened up before the poet, which he needs in order to reach the richness of all things.' He thus defended 'despotism', for it created great character: 'an intelligent, calm overview, rigorous activity, steadfastness, decisiveness, are all qualities that one needs to serve the despot, for they help to develop men with able minds who then obtain the first positions of the State where they learn to be rulers.'[11]

Katharina Mommsen has stressed that since Goethe, 'it has become usual in Europe to see the two worlds of the Ancient and Orient as standing beside each other with equal rights.' At any rate, it cannot escape today's observer that for the prince of poets as for many subsequent romantic poets, the idealised and now long-forgotten world of the 'classical Orient' – that of the early days of the Bedouin-Arab or the Persian Middle Ages where Hafiz lived – was significantly closer than the *real Orient* of their time. The transfiguration of the mythical Islamic *past* was expressed by them in rapture for the 'unspent morality' of an imaginary and archaic early period. This contrasted vividly with the rather more negative or indifferent valuation of the *contemporary* Orient, that of the prevailing political might of the Ottoman empire, which in fact continued to 'subjugate' the 'classical Arab legacy' in the areas where Islam originated.

In the first half of the nineteenth century, none of the European poets gripped by the romantic 'Orient fever' turned their attention to the contemporary poetical creations of Turkish-Ottoman literature. They translated, commented on and adapted 'unspoilt' Persian and Arab works from the early days of Islam, whose 'consumption' was apparently considered to be worthy of recommendation only from a greater historical distance.

In 1834 the Orientalist G. Flügel, a connoisseur of all three 'Islamic literatures', put forward another plausible reason for the lack of Western interest in the cultural achievements of the tangible Ottoman presence:

> the lot of [the Turkish language] was the same as that of the other two Oriental languages, as regards the lack of a reason to study them: no old Turkish translation of the *Holy Scriptures* [the Bible] existed, and so nothing towards the explanation of the Bible could be gained from an understanding of Turkish.[12]

The reference to the absence of renderings of the Bible (although they were not entirely lacking) can definitely be taken seriously as a reason for the lack of interest in Turkish-Ottoman language and literature by many a post-Enlightenment devout Christian romantic of the early nineteenth century.

In his *Noten und Abhandlungen* Goethe was able effortlessly to expand his universalist religious beliefs to include Islam. He wrote:

> The only, true and most profound issue in the history of the world and mankind, to which all else is inferior, is and remains the conflict between faith and lack of faith. All epochs where faith prevails, in whatever form it is manifest, are radiant, uplifting and fruitful for the people of the time and for posterity. By contrast, all epochs where lack of faith, whatever form it takes, claims a miserable victory, even though they may shine forth with an illusory radiance momentarily, disappear from posterity, for no one wishes to trouble themselves with a discovery of the barren.

He pleaded for a form of 'sceptical mobility' in the face of *all* dogmatism and delimitation; although, as was later interpreted, he wanted to depict 'neither the East nor the West, but rather Man, whom he discovered intuitively here as there'.

The subsequent generation of European 'poets and thinkers' who became interested in the Orient often formulated their image of it under the much greater influence of the topical politics of the day than had the detached representatives of the Enlightenment in the eighteenth century, with their aloof and idealising approach to the critique of the Orient and Islam.

## The French Occupation of Egypt and its Ideological Consequences in Europe

On 2 July 1798, a French expedition of 30,000 men landed in Egypt under the command of Napoleon Bonaparte. Alexandria fell the same day after little resistance, and three weeks later Napoleon's victorious troops had already occupied the capital city of Cairo. In the course of the French Republic's clashes with England, the most important thing for the French was to hit the British empire at one of its weakest points: the Motherland's connection to India. However, Napoleon's ambitions went further: he dreamed of establishing a great Oriental empire, including India.

This campaign marked the beginning of a period of colonial interest in the Middle East and constituted a first successful attack on the weakened Ottoman empire, under whose nominal supremacy Egypt still found itself. Shortly after, however, the landing of the joint Anglo-Ottoman forces resulted in a military turning point leading to victory over the French fleet at Aboukir and the retreat of the French from Egypt in 1801. Yet the French venture nonetheless represented a significant break in the political and cultural relationships between Europe and the Orient. From the point of view of the West, it appeared that Napoleon (and with him France, which was still being shaped by the radical changes of the Revolution) had decided that with his invasion of Egypt he was after 'world domination'. For the Islamic world – particularly for the Ottoman rulers – this incursion into one of its heartlands by a Western army was a shock, and caused panic and confusion among a people who had never been subject to a European threat throughout Ottoman rule.

'The greatest cavalry of the Orient, perhaps that of the whole earth', as the French campaign's chronicler Dominique Virant Denon triumphantly notes in his description of the Battle at the Pyramids, 'the pride of the Mamelukes has been crushed on the bayonets of our infantry. A small troop of Frenchmen under the command of a hero have at this moment conquered a continent and an empire has received another lord.'[13] The political skill of General Bonaparte (in August 1799 he secretly broke through the English naval blockade, leaving his troops behind, returning home to France a 'victor') and Denon's magnificently illustrated accounts of his military deeds and the cultural treasures of the 'conquered', which appeared in luxurious editions, helped to transform Napoleon's decisive defeat into a brilliant public relations victory 'in the eyes of the world', of Europe and the Orient, and Bonaparte was celebrated as the 'conqueror of Egypt'.[14]

Even Heinrich Heine was among the many enthusiastic admirers of this venture. Twenty years later, the memory of it still thrilled him in his *Englische Fragmente*:

> [Napoleon's] name is like a herald from the ancient world and is as ancient and heroic as the names of Alexander and Caesar. He has become a byword among the people, and when the Orient and the Occident meet, then they will come to understand each other through this unique name.[15]

The emperor's biographers gave him to understand that 'he has been able to gain the respect and admiration of a large portion of the native [Egyptian] population' and he went so far as to confer on Napoleon the 'rank of a world Messiah'. After the emperor's death in exile in 1821, Heine wrote: 'And St Helena is the holy grave where the peoples of the Orient and Occident go on pilgrimage in ships with colourful pennants and take courage from the great memories of the deeds of the world's Saviour!' The liberal intellectual Heine, who considered himself a 'freedom fighter' and 'friend of the revolution', a critical observer of the political conditions in conservative Germany who never tired of denouncing the anti-Semitism there, clung to his ideal of Napoleon as the saviour from the West who would unite the people, a mediator between the Orient and the Occident, with effusive and apparently naive enthusiasm.

Following the Egypt fever that broke out in Europe after the French adventure, Heine too began to take a greater interest in this country. He even planned, but never undertook, a trip there (because 'the obelisks in Paris weren't enough'). Apart from his enthusiasm for a largely imaginary 'antiquity' of Egypt, he cultivated a fairly conventional picture of the Orient (like the majority of his European contemporaries), notable for its stereotyped prejudices and vague passion for the past poetic and unspoilt 'classical Islamic period' in contrast to the real Orient (in the form of Ottoman power) – just as it had been cherished in Goethe's time.

The poet and publicist was hardly enthusiastic about the 'philhellenism' with which Europe was aglow during the Greek efforts to gain independence from the Ottoman empire in the 1820s. The Jew Heine did not warm to the ditties that appeared in newspapers and weekly gazettes all too often in 1821: 'Plant the symbol of faith on 'Stanbul's wall!/ The crescent to the cross must fall,/ The Barbarian to the Greek.' He was indifferent to the religious aspect of the battle between the Greeks and Turks. According to the Heine scholar Fendri, the young, liberally educated and sensitive poet could not identify with a tendency in which the cross (in whose name believers of other religions were despised and not tolerated) was assigned a leading role, and whose followers included fanatics and demagogues of all colours.[16]

To the poet, the conflict between Greeks and Turks appeared to be part of 'mankind's war of liberation' within the framework of cosmopolitan ideas of progress. Turkey, a repressive political creation with archaic power structures, was a natural enemy for him. A religious agnostic, he did not limit his contempt of Turkey to a condemnation of Ottoman politics, for he discerned in 'the Turk' a fanatical hatred for people of different faiths whether Jews or Christians: 'for both creeds are hated by him, he looks upon them as dogs and gives them this honourable title as well'. At the outbreak of war between Russia and the Ottoman empire, he celebrated the Russian Tsar Nicholas I as avenger of the Greeks, 'the knight of Europe who protects Greek widows and orphans from the Asiatic barbarians'. This highly questionable assessment lacks no common, contemporary cliché about the non-European Orient, with its different creed, as a reality in Turkey. In 1840, Heine still merely showed a somewhat grudging respect for the slightly nebulous 'genius of the Arabs', which had 'never died completely, but had only fallen asleep in the quiet life of the Bedouin. Perhaps the Arabs are only awaiting the right call in order to storm out as before from their sultry wastelands, refreshed by sleep.'

However unoriginal cosmopolitan Heine's image of the Orient might appear to be in comparison to those of his conservative, Christian romantic contemporaries, it did differ from the old conceptions of the eighteenth century in one significant respect. The *despot*, though exotic, was a nonetheless equal *male* adversary, and a kind of symbol of the earlier view of the Orient. The view of the imaginary Orient that began to take shape in the nineteenth century in the minds of Heine, the romantics and later the symbolists had to a large extent lost its threatening and aggressive features. The idea of a *feminine* Orient began to develop in literature: a dreamworld of rapture, ecstatic visions and sensual pleasures, and notably one where the male fantasy of limitless power over the female body was realised.[17]

According to this interpretation, Heine's image of the Orient is 'feminine' and its symbol is the ideal lover in the form of a 'beautiful, loving, sensuous rose'; among her attributes are 'silence, passivity, childlikeness, irrationality and a dangerous sensuousness, timeless eternity and finally emptiness, in a word strangeness'.[18] These images did not correspond to the realities of Islamic countries, except perhaps in a metaphorical sense. Since the nineteenth century, the age of imperialism, the weaker the Orient appeared to the expansionist endeavours of the West, 'the greater the tendency to depict the relationship between the two hemispheres in terms of the *weak* and *strong sexes'*. Thus, according to Hegel, 'the Asiatic empire's ordained fate' was 'to be subject to the Europeans': the role of the Orient had already been determined as 'the passive object of conquest'.[19]

Equally characterised by images of a feminine Orient were the observations of the utopian socialist movement of the Saint-Simonists in the 1830s. They hoped for a 'peaceful unification of the active, restless and dynamic Occident with the passive, introspective Orient' and, in all seriousness, for some form of 'salvation of mankind'. In 1833, a few of them travelled to the East (to Istanbul and Egypt) in the hope of fulfilling this vision of the future. They went to look for a 'Mère supreme' or female incarnation of the Messiah, a 'Femme-Messie' who would ascend the throne beside the 'Père Supreme' – Prosper Enfantin, the quasi-religious leader of the Saint-Simonists – in order to work with him for the salvation of mankind in the East and West.[20] The strange plan failed because they could not find such a 'Femme-Messie' in the Orient, but it gives us some indication of the degree of obsession that the mania of projected exotic femininity assumed, even in a socio-political movement that Heinrich Heine had long considered 'the most progressive party for the emancipation of the people'.[21] In nineteenth-century literature, art and music, many mythical or pseudo-historical heroines, from Aida, Judith and Delilah to Salome, personified a fascination with the imaginary Orient, each one a 'symbol of the "wild", undomesticated human being'. While writers, painters and musicians often set the dreamy fantastical desires and expectations of the West in a distant past, in everyday politics (as with the Saint-Simonists) a similar notion 'determined the colonial sphere: they crystallised into a *mythology* of imperialism, modelled on the contemporary battle of the sexes.'[22]

Nineteenth-century knowledge-seeking travellers, Orientalists and archaeologists added 'elements of reality' to this picture of Islamic countries which increasingly nurtured the European public with images of an authentic and contemporary Orient alongside the dreamworld of fantasy.

As the master of the creation of such a trivialised and apparently 'tangible' Middle East, Karl May (1842–1912) is unrivalled in his ability to capture the 'Wild Islamic East' of Turkey, Kurdistan and Arabia similar to the 'Wild West' of America – in his multi-volume adventure stories.[23] Although they are devoid of all sensuousness, eroticism or ambiguous sensuality, they are unambiguous in the simplicity of his prejudices and in his Wilhelminian Teutonic swashbuckling (with not only anti-Islamic, but also anti-French, anti-British and anti-Semitic tendencies). May's fictitious portrayals were supposed to convey a semblance of the probable. They are nonetheless images of an 'Orient of European self-portrayal' (K.U. Syndram) of places where dreams for which there is no other home can be realised.[24] His Eastern scenario seems so distinctive, above all, because it provides the setting for the German sense of mission and the strong-arm tactics of the years of the *Gründerzeit* (the era of industrial expansion after 1871). Here too, the Orient functions 'as a stage set for European (i.e. German) actors, and thus as a mirror of Western views'.

The great inability and unwillingness of European observers to pay as much attention to the Islamic East, its realities and contemporary manifestations as they lavished on its fancifully idealised 'mythical' past can be traced throughout the nineteenth century. The paradoxical relationship of the Occident with the 'land of the East' since the eighteenth century was marked by the projection of their own European spiritual and political processes of development (be it in a positive or negative sense) on to the 'counter-world' of the Orient, which was fascinating but remained foreign and 'different'. The detachment and reserve towards a region which was just 'not Europe' have never been overcome. The basic position of the Europeans was recently defined thus: Europe's efforts to reassure itself have traditionally been directed at the East or the Orient and until today it continues to find its antithesis there. This helps it in its self-assertion as the leading world civilisation.[25] That this fundamental Western construct should have its antithesis in the Middle Eastern view of the West as the 'anti-Orient' can be regarded as an almost natural truism, just as it can also be considered certain that the 'Oriental' identity considers itself to be based mainly on an antithesis to the West. The belated process of modernisation in the Islamic world hesitantly set in motion in the nineteenth century was due in the first place to the confrontation with the 'enlightened West', and could be ascribed to the superficial Westernising influence of the epoch-making invasion by Napoleon and his army in Egypt, and its devastating effects on the way the Ottoman empire saw itself.[26]

## The Phase of Modernisation in the Nineteenth Century

Of the French Revolution, the well-known scholar Bernard Lewis says:

> With the French Revolution, for the first time, we find a great movement of ideas penetrating the barrier that separated the House of War from the House of Islam, finding a ready welcome among Muslim leaders and thinkers, and affecting to a greater or lesser degree every layer of Muslim society.[27]

The eighteenth century saw a number of attempts at military reform in the Ottoman empire (after several disastrous defeats in wars with Venice, Austria and Russia). With the support of the French, sections of the traditional troops were reorganised by introducing new training methods for the artillery, and setting up engineering and training schools in the sciences and mathematics, run by French instructors who taught in French with the help of interpreters. The Orient gained gradual access to Western scientific knowledge and new technology in the century of European Enlightenment primarily via French experts, engineers and officers.

It has often been emphasised that various attempts at reform during the centuries of political and military decline of the Ottoman empire were only undertaken 'half-heartedly'. Large sections of the elite representing the interests of the state interpreted the growing European superiority as merely one of technical progress and know-how. The spiritual and ideological processes of change in the European states were either ignored or disapproved of.

A return to the 'Golden Age' of the beginnings of the Ottoman empire with regained military power, as well as the achievement of the uninterrupted supremacy of a theocratic Islamic state, were proclaimed as the aim of efforts to become acquainted with Western knowledge and methods in the field of military engineering.

Thus, until 1789, the process of the Orient's opening up to Europe in the technological arena on the one hand, and to spiritual and political changes on the other, was not parallel but strongly asynchronous (by about 100 years). However, the change in Ottoman diplomacy, from *unilateral* into reciprocal, a reform which coincided with the events of the French Revolution, could be interpreted as the expression (if somewhat belated) of the Ottoman leadership's readiness to come to terms, in the cultural and political arena, with the European countries who were usually militarily victorious. This important change in interstate relations made it possible for the Ottoman government to obtain the direct and continuous information on political events in Europe that it had lacked until the 1790s.

Until this point, the Ottoman empire (like all other Islamic states previously), had done without *permanent* diplomatic representation in the capitals of foreign powers. According to its self-image, determined by classical Islamic concepts of state, and guided in all matters in the best possible way by the principles of religious law, the Ottoman empire considered itself superior in principle to all non-Islamic forms of government. Constant and regular relations between Muslims and non-Muslims who were considered inferior were therefore not considered necessary, and there was little incentive to develop permanent diplomatic contacts as had been customary in Europe since the Renaissance. For these reasons, an *ad hoc* form of diplomacy existed, and the odd mission to Europe and everyday business were carried out through the permanent diplomatic representations of the foreign powers in Istanbul. Local Christian interpreters were responsible for verbal communication, as hardly any high-ranking Ottoman official or dignitary at the time spoke a Western language or had direct experience of Europe.

The recognition that permanent diplomatic contacts and competent, so to speak on-the-spot, analyses of political developments in Europe would help reduce the dangerous lack of information and knowledge, led the reformist Sultan Selim III (1789–1808) to establish embassies in the important capital cities of Europe in 1792. The first was set up in London (1793), followed shortly by Berlin and Vienna, and finally Paris in 1796. Among other things, Ottoman ambassadors were instructed to 'study the countries they were accredited in, and to acquire knowledge of the language and general knowledge of the corresponding countries that could be of use to their state', as is stated in a decree.

Selim's measures for reform were often criticised as being too little, too late. Indeed, the changeover to diplomatic communication was introduced just at the time when the events of the French Revolution and the turmoil of the Napoleonic Wars had led to a temporary collapse of the diplomatic system. Moreover, the inefficient and confused bureaucracy of the Sublime Porte (the seat of the Ottoman government) turned out be unable adequately to evaluate and catalogue all the wealth of new findings and impressions that came in from reports, secret dispatches and memoranda.

The fact that Sultan Selim opened the first embassy in England, not in France, in 1793, must be considered in the light of the turmoil of the Revolution and the subsequent unstable political situation in

France. Civil servants adequately familiar with the political situation and diplomatic practices in Europe were not available to the Porte as diplomats. Most of the first ambassadors were palace or chancellery officials of the old school who came from the traditional *ulema*, and were classical Islamic scholars who had no knowledge whatsoever of Western languages.

Between 1797 and 1811, the Porte sent three 'permanent ambassadors' to Paris. None of them learned a word of French and all were dependent on interpreters (mostly Greek) for their information. Apart from commenting on current Napoleonic politics in their diplomatic correspondence, they also continually commented on its past history, the French Revolution, whose aims, in their evaluation, were still being pursued by Napoleon.

It would appear that in the Islamic world, a real examination of the meaning of the phenomenon of revolution only began at this point. While it had long been considered an internal matter for the French, or at most one with serious repercussions for Christian Europe, because of the Revolutionary Wars, compounded by Napoleon's invasion of Egypt in 1798, it turned out to be a threat to the interests of the Islamic countries themselves.

The disturbing and disconcerting news from the diplomats in Paris led to a memorandum presented to Selim III in 1798 by one of his advisers, explaining the occurrences in Europe and warning that

> The infamous atheists Voltaire and Rousseau and other 'materialists' had written and publicised various leaflets in which they had offended and slandered the pure Prophet and the great Ruler. They had spoken of getting rid of all religions and made allusions to the enjoyment of Equality and Republicanism. Tempted by the lure of the New, many people, even women and children had turned to them ... such that heresy and malice had spread through their minds like syphilis and destroyed their faith. As the Revolution had progressed, the sinners had not shrunk from closing the churches, murdering their monks or driving them away. They had set their hearts on *Equality* and *Freedom*, from which they hoped for salvation in this world ... At the same time, it is well known that order and the continuance of the State are based on the foundation of the law of religion and its teachings.[28]

In 1802 the ambassador in Paris reported that rabble-rousers in France had removed all necessary fear of God and respect for his laws among the people. Instead they had drawn up a rebellious declaration called 'The Rights of Man and the Citizen', printed it everywhere, translated it into all languages in order to spur the simple peoples of all countries and religions into revolt against their rulers.

And in 1808:

> They pronounce the books the Prophets brought us, a great mistake, and hold the Qur'an, Torah and the Psalms to be lies and useless prattle ... and that all are equal as people; no one was superior to another by virtue of his income, and everyone should provide for themselves in this life. They make empty promises to everyone ... and have joined forces under Satan's banner.

The judgements of the three ambassadors in their reports sent over a period of several years, are in essential agreement: they criticise one element of the political development of France from 1798 onwards: *secularism*; and with it the separation of church and state, the abandonment of all religious teachings, the cult of reason, and the proclamation of individual freedom and equality.

The unanimous criticism by the envoys to France was soon officially circulated in the official historiography of the Ottomans. It was considered legitimate for an Islamic state to acquire a knowledge of Western science and technology in order to reinstate the former glory of a previously politically and militarily powerful state. After all, that is how the Russian empire was revived under Peter the Great. At the same time, however, one had to be wary of the friendship of the Christians, their falseness and their treacherous aims. They strove only to *ruin Islam*, to abolish religions and the true teachings of the Prophet. They also confused the hearts and minds of youth in order to teach them their language and customs, to sow the seed of godlessness in their hearts and to undermine the principles of the religious laws (the Sharia). The rebellious proclamations of the equality between rich and poor and of freedom served them in this.

The chronicler Asim Efendi attributes Selim III's downfall to the harmful influence of France on his policies and to his 'zeal for innovation'. The criticism that the deposed and murdered ruler did not maintain the distinction between 'acceptable' Western knowledge (in the fields of engineering and the military) and the unacceptable (godless and un-Islamic) body of thought is implicit.

One central concept arises constantly in the above-mentioned diplomatic criticism of Europe and in the official historiography of those years: *freedom* (Arabic: *hurriyah*). This term underwent an interesting change in meaning precisely during the time of the French Revolution and its aftermath. Before 1800 this word was primarily a legal term in the Islamic languages, meaning the absence of or the opposite of slavery. In the course of the nineteenth century, following the events in Europe, the term assumed a new political dimension that many contemporary Islamic authors found unacceptable. Thus they did not use the word in the sense of *freedom*, but as 'libertinism', 'excess' or 'anarchy'. This is the case in the writings mentioned above against the aims of the Revolution: the common people were being ruined by promises of libertinism and egalitarianism.

It is only many years later, in 1815, that the concept of 'freedom' is used with a positive Islamic connotation when an early scholar of reform and historian, Shanizade, who unusually was also a polyglot in Western languages, discusses the advantages of European parliamentarianism in his writings.[29] However, he presented this institution to his audience as a traditional Islamic institution, a forum for open discussion followed by constructive decisions: for *free* debates among representatives from the people who take part in the decision-making process. An echo of the events of 1789 and its consequences is to be seen in the modified formulation adapted for the Islamic reader. Innovations and new ideas were often heralded in two ways in the traditional Islamic world: they were either vehemently disputed (or fought against) or they were traced back to a supposedly Islamic origin and were thus able to be adapted with no problem. It was no different in the Ottoman empire.

The establishment of 'permanent diplomatic representations' in the capitals of Europe signified a considerable step towards the fundamental and institutional opening up of the Islamic world to the West, which was gradually to influence the structural reorganisation of politics and society in the Orient in the nineteenth century. As a result of internal political tensions with opponents of reform, however, no further ambassador was accredited in Paris after 1811. In the other European capitals 'permanent diplomacy' was also practically frozen, and the residences were merely maintained at a lower level by *chargés d'affaires*, who were almost exclusively Greek subjects of the Ottoman empire. In reaction to the Greek uprising of 1821 and the European position in this regard, Sultan Mahmud II gave up this solution as well, and did without permanent diplomatic representation abroad for more than ten years (until 1834).

Although contact with Europe, at any rate diplomatic contact, was curtailed during this phase, interest in reform did not stagnate in any way. Instead, it resulted in processes of structural reorientation, which ultimately led to the proclamation of the Gülhane decree of reform in 1839, a declaration of limited civil rights and freedoms in the entire Ottoman empire. A considerable part was played in this by the creation of an institution which had far-reaching implications for the belated process of modernisation: the Imperial Training Institute for Translation founded in 1821 was the first of its kind in the entire Islamic East (in 1837 a similar institution came into being in Egypt). This establishment served the reform-orientated education of the civil service and the schooling in foreign languages of a new Ottoman diplomatic corps that no longer had to rely on the support of Greek (or other non-Muslim ) interpreters. The learned and linguistically proficient historian Shanizade was also involved in the organisation of this institution. His interpretation of *hurriyah* to mean 'individual freedom' finally found its way into the 1839 edict of reform. This concept, temporarily labelled as negative, given the background of the negative view of the French Revolution and its ideals in Islamic countries, was fully rehabilitated in the Gülhane decree. It is twice mentioned in the decree which initiated the greatest legislative process of reorganisation in the Orient in the nineteenth century: 'Every man shall *freely* be in charge of his property'; and 'Assemblies shall be gathered where everyone can *freely* represent their ideas and observations without hindrance.'[30]

This is the 'bourgeois' Ottoman interpretation of a concept that had triggered so much fear and resentment at the outbreak of the Revolution a half-century earlier. Beside the belief that diplomats specially educated for their stay in Europe and with a knowledge of Western languages were the right people to convey information on political developments abroad, it soon became customary to send groups of younger scholarship-holders to the West, so that they might learn about the latest developments in European science and technology and convey them to the non-religious institutes in their homelands. The former Ottoman Governor of Egypt, Muhammad Ali Pasha, who succeeded in being recognised by the Sublime Porte in Istanbul as viceroy of the country in 1805, and who proved to be an ambitious rival for the Ottoman sultan in the process of modernisation on the Western model, was the first Islamic ruler to send a delegation of students to Italy in 1809. The Ottomans followed his example in 1827.

## From Rifa'a al-Tahtawi to the Supremacy of European Colonialism

What the French call 'Freedom' and strive for as such, is exactly that what we Muslims describe as 'justice' and 'fairness' in as far as the relationship between Power and Freedom is synonymous with the creation of equality in Law and Justice, so that the Ruler cannot suppress anyone. It is the *Laws* that have been made the Ruler and guiding principle in France.

This remarkably enthusiastic verdict from the pen of an Egyptian author is on the situation in France after the Revolution – admittedly not that of 1789 but the July Revolution of 1830. It was found in a travelogue printed four years later in Cairo and represents a milestone in the history of Egypt's modernisation.[31]

Its author, the scholarly young al-Azhar-Sheikh Rifa'a al-Tahtawi (1801–73), belonged to the first delegation of students sent to France by the reformer Muhammad Ali after Egypt broke away from the Ottoman empire (1811), to learn foreign languages and skills in European science and technology. Forty-four scholarship students spent five years from 1826 to 1831 in Paris, on the orders of the Egyptian ruler in order to acquaint themselves with the latest developments there.

The young theologist Tahtawi, sent by his reform-minded monarch to France for five years of study, represented a new generation of Muslim intellectuals. In the first decade of the nineteenth century, the ruling classes of the Ottoman empire and Egypt, the two Islamic countries which felt the collision with the vastly technologically and militarily superior Europe most acutely, had arrived at new insights and strategies: the process of modernisation and renewal in both of these rival states was to be advanced only with the help of native experts and specialists educated in the West. A knowledge of European languages was considered the key to success with which Western progress was to be achieved.

Thus, Tahtawi, whose linguistic talents were soon evident, was chosen by the leader of the first mission of students to Europe to study French intensively, although as a theologist he was originally intended as spiritual adviser to the delegation. Tahtawi applied himself to his new task with dedication during his five years in Paris and for the rest of his life. He was the only 'student of the humanities' among his colleagues who were working on the latest developments in military technology and the natural sciences. His great passion for the language and literature of his host country enabled him to have more intimate access to the developments in France than his fellow students; he was interested in all aspects of the social and political life of Paris, and all are given sensitive and almost objective treatment in his account.

With a sense of moderation, composure and indeed alacrity remarkable in a traditionally educated Muslim, he also described for the readership of his native country phenomena that belonged to the taboos or stereotypical prejudices about the West: the religious indifference of wide sections of society in Paris and their contempt for the bigoted clergy, as well as the consumption of alcohol among the French, which according to his observations had less to do with excess than with the cheerful homeliness of the various social gatherings.

Tahtawi, well-versed in and a lover of Oriental literature, spoke with a subtle irony surprising in an Islamic theologian. He did not consider French *belles–lettres* (easily accessible to him through avid study) 'wicked', but now and again he did miss the formal skills coupled with the hidden meanings and ambiguity of content found in Oriental literature. Why was it that the French sang the praises of the wine they so treasured with such crude directness and unimaginative simplicity? Why had they found only *one* name for this elixir, this medium for which the traditional Muslim, be he a mystic ascetic or epicure, had found so many different metaphors? Tahtawi noted this with somewhat condescending astonishment.

Tahtawi's complete account of his stay in Paris is nonetheless characterised by an undeniable admiration for the French. To a certain extent he even considered them to be the closest people to the Arabs in things that matter most – 'in matters of honour, freedom and pride' – the highest praise an Egyptian could give.

Tahtawi's cautious attempt at a different interpretation in the 1830s is even more remarkable when considered against the background of decades of unanimous condemnation of the radical and revolutionary changes in Europe by the Islamic world. The continued stay of young Oriental diplomats and students in Europe, and the knowledge of Western languages, norms and ideas which had been considered either mysterious or abhorrent until then brought about a gradual revision of the condemnation of Revolution in the West that had at first seemed total.

Opinions such as those expressed in Tahtawi's account of 1834 contributed considerably to the new evaluation of the West. Several editions of his book were published and it was prescribed as compulsory reading for civil servants in Egypt's state schools by the reformist ruler Muhammad Ali.

Highly respected as a cultural reformer, Tahtawi saw shortly before his death in 1873 the establishment of an institution he had long fought for: schools for Muslim girls in Egypt. But his native country was shortly to confront the other face of the European ideal of Revolution: imperialism. For Egypt, this meant the British occupation of the country in 1882.

As principal of the Madrasat al-Sunnah (Language School) founded in Cairo in 1837 (modelled on the Ottoman Imperial Institute for Translation), al-Tahtawi had seen to the introduction of a syllabus which encompassed much more than language teaching. He included history, geography and mathematics, as well as Islamic and French law. The combination of European and indigenous knowledge made the school the only institution in the Orient (apart from its counterpart in Istanbul) where not only a narrow and traditional knowledge but a worldly 'education' was imparted. In its fourteen years of existence, the school produced a large number of graduates who contributed to the intellectual renewal of their country as teachers and translators who were to make up Egypt's new intellectual elite in the second half of the nineteenth century.[32]

In Cairo as in Istanbul – the main centres of reform on the Western model – the translation and publication of Western books in the first few decades of the century was of central significance. Over 240 books were printed between 1822 and 1842 within the framework of a programme financed by the state, most of them translations into Turkish. For in the time of Muhammad Ali Pasha's rule, this was the language of Egypt's ruling elite, for whom works on military science and navigation as well as mathematics were published. Over half of the scholarship students Muhammad Ali sent to Europe were Turkish-speaking Ottomans. Even the few books of historical content that were translated from European languages were reserved for the Turkish-speaking classes. On the other hand, works on human and veterinary medicine and agriculture appeared in Arabic, as they were not intended for the ruling class.

The Egyptian translations into Turkish were also distributed in the Ottoman empire and reprinted in Istanbul. Until the middle of the century, translation programmes there had been limited to scientific works, while publications of historical or literary content were contemplated much later than in Egypt.[33]

Nonetheless, the time of 'civil' reforms in the Ottoman empire (the Tanzimat-i khayriyah, 'Beneficent Reordering') from 1839 to 1876, the years of Muhammad Ali Pasha's and his successor's rule until the British occupation of Egypt in 1882, were as much shaped by the intellectual opening up of both countries towards Western scientific knowledge and technological innovation as they were influenced by contemporary intellectual and political trends. Debates on parliamentarianism and constitutional monarchy, individual rights and freedom of the press were among them and had an entirely ambivalent effect. As Bernard Lewis has said, the process of Oriental–Western exchange of ideas and influences had become irreversible. In the second half of the century, the number of Muslims attracted to the European capitals grew constantly for the most varied of reasons: at first it was diplomats followed by the scholarship students, and after a time political refugees came from the empire of the Ottoman sultans as well as from Egypt.[34]

Muhammad Ali's successors held on to his motto of wanting to make the land on the Nile 'a part of Europe'. The ambitious plans for reform, including the Suez Canal opened in 1869 with much pomp and ceremony, and long-term, severely debt-laden investments which made the country dependent on the West to the tune of nearly £100 million in 1876, made the internal situation continually more precarious through reckless tax increases and other repressive measures undertaken under the Khedive Ismail. In a desperate attempt to save the state from bankruptcy, Ismail sought out the main creditor countries, England and France, to agree to a system of joint budgetary supervision ('dual control'). This failed and finally led to his deposition in 1879 and to the British occupation of Egypt three years later – a dictatorial rule which was to last seventy years.

On the other hand, the conflict between the authority of the state and the press and representatives of constitutionalism on whom censorship and restrictions were imposed was aggravated by internal political tensions in the country. These clashes in turn became a reason for the Khedive's 'appeal for help' to the British, and why many political opponents were driven to exile in Europe.

To an even greater degree, this was the reason for the developments in the Ottoman empire in the 1860s and 1870s. The graduates of the new educational establishments which had followed the Tanzimat reforms formed the opposition. They demanded that the modernisation of the state be accompanied by general social reform, that the traditional autocratic position of the sultan and his ruling class be replaced by a new constitutional system which would give the subjects the possibility of sharing power with the rulers, and that the power of the governing be limited by a parliament and a constitution. This opposition movement, which was supported mainly by the literati and intellectuals, operated under the name 'Young Ottomans'.[35] Many of their publications could only be printed abroad where many of their representatives had fled into exile. Among them were writers and publicists such as Ziya Pasha and Namik Kemal, who later became so famous and influential. Their critiques appeared abroad in English and French, and for the time being limited editions in Turkish reached only a small number of the educated in the Ottoman state.

## Wilhelm II as 'Patron of the Mohammedans'

The disappointed reformers of the first and second generations had to realise that the ideals of a new education characterised by Western ideas would, in the face of a repressive political reality pressurised by European imperialism, remain mere wastepaper in states such as Egypt or the Ottoman empire. Bitterly, they often chose the path of European exile. Paris and London were preferred destinations, and Geneva was also attractive to the francophone liberal opposition.

Few went to German-speaking areas. Until the 1870s this corresponded with the status and nature of Prussian–Ottoman relations. Since the 1830s, German military advisers had from time to time assisted with the reorganisation of the Ottoman army, but cultural and economic relations were well behind those with the other great European powers in these years.

In the 1880s, Wilhelm II thought it necessary to compensate for Germany's tardiness in active Oriental politics, and his sense of mission twice led him to the Ottoman empire in 1889 and 1898. In November 1898 he went to Damascus where he presented himself as 'the patron of 300 million Mohammedans' and 'the constant friend of the Sultan, their Caliph'.

The main aim of the rapprochement with the Ottoman empire sought by German politicians appears to have been the possibility of exerting immense economic influence. The Baghdad railway project, which was to link Central Europe to Iraq via Istanbul, Ankara and Syria, and which was transferred to two German concessionaries in 1888 and 1903 (under the Deutsche Bank's control), was seen by both sides as the showpiece of the new collaboration.

In the host of publications devoted to the Baghdad railway project there is no dearth of contemporary German accounts at pains to emphasise the purely commercial nature of this huge enterprise, although their arguments and choice of words speak for themselves and barely conceal that the opposite was the truth:[36]

Germany does not seek to conquer the Orient or to expand her territory, she wishes to trade with Turkey and Turkish Asia, build roads and railways, provide and receive work, exchange and acquire goods, to earn, achieve and spread usufruct and prosperity. The operation of the German railway will surely make the locomotive the most effective 'educator' in the distant East.

Like a thunderous echo she booms out an awakening call through the land of the East. Her iron bulk resounds like the clash of swords. Like the surge of waves, her clouds of steam rise up to the glowing firmament. With furious speed she completes her journey. Visionary, reliable as the movement of the stars, day in day out, the Asian sees the locomotive bursting forth from the distant reaches of his horizon, and disappearing from his sight into the distant horizon. Where do these houses on wheels filled with strange men come from? Where do they go? Why this mad flight? *Alla franca* it is not, for even the great 'Napliun', on whose authority the meagre bit of Europeanness of the Orient has relied for over a century, was never capable of this. *'Min Alemannia'* – from Germany! reply the Turks and Arabs reverently. And the Asian senses that he has missed an entire world in dream and sleep, and that for him the time has now come to tear the treacherous blindfold of fatalism from his eyes, and to join the circle of the great nations of the West, who believe in Freedom and the power of self-determination, and have in this surpassed themselves in their power throughout the world. From this moment of discovery, however, victory over the Asian has been achieved, and Europe's cultural circle has grown by another twenty million people, the one-time paradise has been opened up for a new Germanic migration!

Already the steam traffic rudely but irresistibly shakes the Anatolian from his deadly rut and ... its piercing whistle drives the Arab and the Kurd from the keif that pierces nothing: *Karavapor beklemes!* The train won't wait! *Chabuk gitmeli!* Forward![37]

Let us look more closely at the contemporary German popular image of the Orient, or rather of the Ottoman empire, as it was circulated shortly before and after the turn of the century. In the press, the more or less discriminating historical or geographical journalistic press which was supposed to convey a 'broadened horizon' and understanding of the new political and economic situations (entirely accepting traditional social and societal structures), the following could be read, for example:

> If I am to comment on the current view of the harmfulness of *Polygamy* for society and state, then I must admit that I consider it to be greatly overestimated ... It promotes able individuals to obtain desirable offspring, it creates a valuable dam (along with early marriage) against the spread of venereal disease, renders the ugly type of old maid, so common amongst us, almost unknown, and raises the man's wellbeing, that is to say of that part of humankind who usually earns a living for the family, and is responsible for spiritual and material progress on earth, and may therefore make greater demands.

To answer the above-mentioned questions in a nutshell, I see myself forced to declare that Oriental society is *favourably* influenced by the present position of women.

In short, I am forced to the conclusion that the social position of Oriental women is entirely appropriate, that it contributes essentially to the strength of family life there and that it is undoubtedly preferable to the ever-increasing over-estimation of women, that is prevalent here as a result of *Anglo-American influences.*

I am fully aware that with my views, I am following a path that deviates not inconsiderably from that of most contributors to this subject, and that I will come up against a certain amount of opposition. But I cannot help exclaiming: *There is no Question about the role of women in the Orient, instead there is an Answer.* They have long since solved the question on the understanding that woman belongs at home and is subordinate to man.[38]

In 1916, during the First World War, Elsa Marquardsen, better known by her maiden name Elsa Sophia von Kamphövener, author of pseudo-Turkish fairytales, gives expression to the contradictory feelings resulting from the current German-Orient engagement:

Disappointment! That is the leitmotif that resounds in a thousand variations from the enthusiastic reflections on the Orient, from the violent, strongly instinctive desire to merge Occidental endeavours with the Oriental ... disappointment, wherever the trader, explorer, politician and soldier might turn ... and yet, the hand of the Turk is worthy of gripping the German hand that holds the sword.[39]

Thus the German 'Orient expert' at the turn of the century shows a refreshing unambiguousness and single-mindedness: now one could well imagine the once fantastically transfigured Islamic world as an economic 'Orient of booty', as explicitly expressed in the thoroughly brusque language of the twentieth century.

The outcome of the First World War had destroyed these dreams, or at least left them to others. Which is not to say that the '*imagerie* of the Orient' will never again, now or in the future, be enriched by further variations of dreams or images of *the enemy.*

# Notes

1   M. Rodinson, *Die Faszination des Islam*, 2nd edn, Munich: Beck Publ., 1991, p. 143.

2   H. Budde and G. Sievernich, in *Europa und der Orient 800–1900*, Munich: Bertelsmann, Lexikon Publ., 1989, p. 15ff.

3   See also, M. Schilling, 'Aspekte des Türkenbildes in Literatur und Publizistik der frühen Neuzeit', *Acta Hohenschwangau 1991*, Munich, 1992, pp. 43–60.

4   Cf. M. E. Pape, 'Turquerie im 18. Jahrhundert und der "Recueil Ferriol"', in *Europa und der Orient*, p. 305ff.

5   Rodinson, *Die Faszination*, p. 68.

6   K.-H. Kohl, 'Cherchez la femme d'Orient', in *Europa und der Orient*, p. 359.

7   On this see in particular K. Mommsen, 'Goethes Bild vom Orient', in W. Hoenerbach (ed.), *Der Orient in der Forschung. Festschrift W. Spies*, Wiesbaden, 1967, pp. 453–70.

8   ibid., p. 462ff.

9   See C. P. Haase, 'Literarische und geschichtliche Wurzeln des Araberbildes der Deutschen', in K. Kaiser and U. Steinbach (eds), *Deutsch-Arabische Beziehungen*, Munich and Vienna, 1981, pp. 205–13.

10   Mommsen, 'Goethes Bild', p. 465.

11   Cf. P. Kappert, 'Vom Übersetzen türkischer Literatur ins Deutsche', in I. Baldauf, K. Kreiser and S. Tezcan (eds), *Türkische Sprachen und Literaturen*, Wiesbaden, 1991, pp. 214ff.

12   Cf. S. Shaw, in G. E. von Grunebaum, *Der Islam II. Fischer Weltgeschichte*, Frankfurt: Fischer Publ., 1971, p. 331ff.

13   D. Syndram, 'Das Erbe der Pharaonen', in *Europa und der Orient*, p. 52ff.

14   D. V. Denon, *Voyage dans la Basse et la Haute Égypte*, Paris, 1802.

15   See M. Fendri, *Halbmond, Kreuz und Schibboleth. Heinrich Heine und der islamische Orient*, Hamburg, 1980, pp. 273ff.

16   ibid., p. 254.

17   Kohl, 'Cherchez la femme', p. 360.

18   Cf. the study by Ch. B. Pfeifer, *Heine und der islamische Orient*, Wiesbaden, 1990.

19   Kohl, 'Cherchez la femme'; cf. also E. Said, *Orientalism*, London: Penguin, 1978, p. 45ff.

20   Fendri, *Halbmond*, p. 288ff.; Kohl, 'Cherchez la femme'.

21   Pfeifer, *Heine und der islamische*, p. 101.

22   Kohl, 'Cherchez la femme', p. 365ff.

23   On him, see A. Marquart, 'Aus Ardistan nach Dschinnistan', in *Exotische Welten – Europäische Phantasien*, Stuttgart, 1987, pp. 78–81.

24   K. U. Syndram, 'Der erfundene Orient in der europäischen Literatur vom 18. bis zum Beginn des 20. Jahrhunderts', in *Europa und der Orient*, p. 340ff.

25   R. Schulze, 'Alte und neue Feindbilder. Das Bild der arabischen Welt und des Islam im Westen', in G. Stein (ed.), *Nachgedanken zum Golfkrieg*, Heidelberg: Palmyra Publ., 1991, p. 256.

26   B. Tibi, *Die Krise des modernen Islam*, Munich, 1981, p. 115.

27   B. Lewis, *The Emergence of Modern Turkey*, 2nd edn, London/Oxford/New York: Oxford University Press, 1968, p. 53.

28   Quotes are from ibid., p. 66ff.

29   The reformer Shanizade (1769–1826) acquired a profound knowledge of Italian, French, Latin and Greek, wrote a study of European medicine and translated several works on anatomy and physiology from Italian into Turkish. His translations mark the end of traditional and the beginning of modern medicine in Turkey; in them he created a new scientific vocabulary which was used till late in to the twentieth century.

30   Cf. the article 'Hurriya' in *Encyclopaedia of Islam III*, 2nd edn, Leiden, 1971, p. 591.

31   His description of his stay in Paris also appeared as a German translation: K. Stowasser (ed. and trans.), *Ein Muslim entdeckt Europa: Rifa'a al-Tahtawi*, Munich, 1989.

32   Cf. ibid., p. 317ff.

33   B. Lewis, *The Muslim Discovery of Europe*, 2nd edn, London,1988, pp. 306ff.

34   ibid., p. 307.

35   Shaw, *Der Islam*, p. 339ff.

36   Cf. P. Kappert, 'Von der Bagdadbahn bis zur Immigration türkischer Gastarbeiterfamilien – zur Geschichte der gegenseitigen Wahrnehmung oder: eine Chronologie der Mißverständnisse', *Acta Hohenschwangau 1991*, pp. 110–26.

37   S. Schneider, *Die Deutsche Bagdad-Bahn und die projectierte Überbrückung des Bosporus in ihrer Bedeutung für Weltwirtschaft und Weltverkehr*, Vienna/Leipzig, 1900, p. 140ff.

38   E. Banse, *Das Orientbuch*, Leipzig, 1914, p. 380ff.

39   E. Marquardsen, *Das Wesen des Osmanen*, Munich, 1916, pp. 3, 78.

# 3

# How Medieval is Islam? Muslim Intellectuals and Modernity

*Reinhard Schulze*

Islamic intellectuals have often seen themselves as the true 'modernisers of modernity'. By this they mean to demonstrate that modernity does not have to represent an antithesis to Islamic identity. Social historical research has indeed been able to show that Islamic societies have their own version of modernity which shares many of its universal aspects but in other respects has also been specifically shaped by Islamic cultural traditions. This chapter will examine the intellectual debate about the 'project' of modernity in Islamic circles. It should be made clear that the inter-Islamic debate on modernity and authenticity (adherence to tradition and purity of origin) conceals a multitude of political positions and world-views which characterise the discourses of a heterogeneous civil Islamic society. So-called 'Islamic fundamentalism' is only a part of this debate; it should not therefore be interpreted as the 'answer to Westernisation' but should be considered part of the contradictory nature of modernity itself.

Among the many statements on Islamic culture is to be found the conviction that the Islamic, and particularly the Arab, world became culturally dependent on the West as a result of the occupation of Egypt by Napoleon Bonaparte in 1798. The principal characteristic of this dependency was the Arab world's borrowing of political ideas, philosophical concepts and scientific ideas from Europe from then on.[1] As a general principle, this statement has serious ramifications for interpretations of the contemporary Islamic world. For every cultural, political or social phenomenon that the Islamic world shares with the West can be seen as a foreign body – an expression of a prolonged process of Westernisation – by those from the West as well as those from the Middle East. The concept of Westernisation is highly political. It allows all attributes of modernity to be defined as European, and Europe or the West to be described as the creator of modernity. The non-European, particularly the Islamic, world is simply cast in the role of the sufferer who was infected by the West's modernity, and can now no longer come to terms with it.[2]

Consequently, modernity is not considered a characteristic of Islamic societies. Instead, it is seen as an integral part of a universal process of becoming civilised. The identification of Europe with 'project modernity', however, prevents modernity from being equally associated with Islamic cultures.[3] Thus, all that remains for the Middle East is a second-hand modernisation, one that is orientated to the West, and is a politically conscious cultural and social reorganisation whose price is almost necessarily the loss of a separate cultural identity.

European control over modernity also makes it difficult for Muslim intellectuals to interpret their own civilisation in a different way to this European point of view. The European primacy over modernity challenges Islamic intellectuals either to justify their adoption of 'project modernity' or vehemently to criticise the same adoption. They appear to be virtually socially destined to this, for after all, according to current theory, intellectuals as a group are themselves a product of the great borrowing from Europe and therefore 'European', and must as a result think in opposition to their own culture.[4]

Both these possible receptions of European modernity are once more the subject of a conflict between two intellectual camps, a subject which has been debated with much ferocity for the last ten years: one camp is made up of Muslim intellectuals who see themselves as champions of modernity *(hadathah / mu'asarah)*.[5] They accept modernity as a universal culture in which Islamic societies should also take part; the European identity of modernity is, however, not questioned. They interpret the Napoleonic occupation of Egypt as a hiatus which prevented any re-establishment of Islamic culture in the Islamic world itself from then onwards. They eagerly take up the contemporary debate on postmodernism *(ma ba'da al-hadatha)*, for therein they see a matter of shared concern for all intellectuals of all modern cultures.[6] In this debate, which has long been popular particularly in North Africa, they see a way out of the dilemma, which presents itself in the negation of their own history and the equally offensive positive assessment of Western modernity.[7]

The other camp is made up of representatives of authenticity *(asalah)* who want to conduct a critique of modernity solely on the basis of Islamic history.[8] They see the historically idealised foundations of Islamic civilisation (and not necessarily of Islamic religion) as the point of reference for a collective identity that in radical thinking should work as an effective negation of modernity.[9] The aim of a process of cultural emancipation would be the recovery of cultural autonomy from the West and the rejection of modernity, sending it back to Europe. Europe alone (the position of this camp could be so paraphrased) would be responsible for the disposal of modernity. The postmodern debate is consistently understood to be a European debate on the failure of modernity. On this point, Islamic intellectuals from the authenticity camp coincide with some neo-conservative critics of modernity in Europe: both sides see themselves as part of a postmodern critique of modernity.

The debate on modernity and authenticity is carried out with sharpened quills; politically, it has so far hardly been effective. The camps have clashed with each other at various writers' congresses or so-called conferences on Islamic thought.[10]

## Criticism of Tradition

The discourse on modernity has strengthened two axioms which are seen in the West as in the East, as basic positions on the Islamic world. The first axiom says that outside Europe or the West modernity can only be understood as a process which causes breaks with and warps tradition. Consequently, the cultural break between tradition and modernity must be induced by Europe. The second axiom is the building block of the evaluation of Islamic tradition itself. It says that Islamic tradition is nothing other than Islam itself, which became reality in the early days of Islam, between 610 and 850. The fundaments of Islamic civilisation were laid down at this time, and are judged positive or negative depending on political standpoint. As a result, both axioms construct a polarised structure which is common to critics and apologists alike. Only the system of values is different.[11]

This construction of Islamic history goes back to the 1840s and 1850s. Since then, the discourse about modernity and authenticity has become so deeply ingrained that accounts of the origin of both positions concerning European cultural dominance over the Orient and the determining role of early Islam have become historical truth. Discussions conducted in academic as in journalistic circles for decades have led to these axioms becoming proven facts. They have structured the contemporary cultural and political debates exactly as they structured the Western view of Islamic societies. The discourse on Islam and modernity is so widely regarded as historical truth that hardly anyone doubts it; moreover it is very useful at present. Hardly anyone questions the fact of the Middle East's feudal dependence on the West. Only in exceptional cases is the history of Islamic societies in the nineteenth century related to their history in the eighteenth century; instead it is simply judged as being the result of

European intervention.[12] And hardly anyone asks how the Napoleonic expeditions to Egypt became a symbol and a factor in an epistemological break which today divides the Islamic world into two camps.

Islamic intellectuals (in a narrow sense, that is those who work in a political Islamic context) have tried from very early on to mediate between authenticity and modernity.[13] The mediation was based on one simple assumption: Islam was the true modernity. Or to overstate the argument: Islam perfected modernity. Such a phrase may at first appear paradoxical, if the very critics of Islamic politics believe that Islam is incompatible with modernity. This phrase, however, conceals a very Islamic tradition of thought which touches on the basis of how Islam is understood. In the Koran itself, Islam is understood as the executor of a historical process. One verse reads 'Today I have perfected your religion for you': this is generally seen as the Prophet Muhammad's final revelation.[14] Islam's historical mission is made clear here: all other religions are to be resolved in Islam, for Islam is the definitive conclusion of God's revelation. Islam thus supersedes all other religions, it is Religion itself.

Of course, Islam shares this feature with all other revealed religions which all see themselves as the last religion. Islam, the youngest and most radical of revelatory religions, particularly stresses this claim: it does not see other religions as false but as distortions of God's revelation. It does not negate earlier religions; instead it absorbs and resolves them. In the last few decades, this point of view has also been applied to new forms of Islamic identity.

Since the eighteenth century, Islamic cultures have also been subject to a strong process of ideologisation, which has led to a far-reaching change in the understanding of Islam. As ideology – and that is the basic common ground of all Islamic politics – Islam is no longer in competition with religions but with ideologies, as for example bourgeois liberalism or socialist and communist ideologies. Just as the religious rivalry between Islam, Christianity and Judaism was seen as a hierarchical system of God's revelation, which found its culmination in Islam, most Islamic intellectuals see their religion as the culmination of an ideological process that has only been imperfectly carried out in Europe. Islam shall perfect these ideologies and render them superfluous. This also means that Islam (as ideology) does not negate other ideologies but absorbs them: Islam is Ideology itself.

With the general decline of ideological world-views in the 1980s, Islamic intellectuals abandoned the pretension of propagating Islamic ideology as the perfection of all others. As an analogy to the gener-

alised debate about modernity, they created a new level of competition: Islam and modernity now faced each other as Islam and
socialism had earlier, or before them Islam and Christianity. And once
again modernity is seen not as the negation of Islam but as its predecessor. All that is not Islamic is necessarily modern, and on the
other hand, all that is truly Islamic perfects the Modern. Consequently,
Islam and modernity did not form an antithesis, but rather a historical
chain: modernity would inevitably flow into Islam.[15]

Such a point of view demands that the discourse over Islam be
aligned with that on modernity. Islam will therefore be as generalised
as the concept of modernity. Islam's religious and new ideological
aspects will retreat into the background in favour of a universalist
understanding which will make Islam a project of civilisation.

The assignment of Islam to modernity is by no means homogenous.
Thus, the role of religion in modernity is judged in different ways.
Many Islamic intellectuals see the danger of their religion receding
behind the demands of civilisation and thus becoming inaccessible
to the broad masses. Overstressing ideas on Islamic civilisation (*al-
tamaddun al-islami*) would create a gap between people's need for
religiosity and the elitist thinking of the intellectuals. The cultural
elite must continue to act as the champion of religion, according to
the Indian scholar Abu al-Hasan Ali an-Nadwi. Religion must always
be a private matter between man and God which must be protected
by the learned. Over emphasising civilisation would nationalise
Muslims' private religiosity and thereby do away with it.

Radical advocates of the philosophy of civilisation – for example,
the Iranian sociologist Ali Shari'ati who died in 1977 and the Egyptian
philosopher Hasan Hanafi – taking a historical-philosophical point
of view – criticise the valuing of Islam as having only an (originally)
religious meaning. This, according to Shari'ati would go directly
against the Islamic concept of the absolute unity of all beings. To
think radically of Islam as a unity demands eliminating the distinction between religion and civilisation. Islam is history's will for
man's perfection in society. With Islamic perfection, history ends.
In this ultimate situation, the separation of the godly and the earthly
will be removed and God will manifest himself in society.

## Islamic Culture in the Civil Society

This specifically teleological definition of Islam is only shared without
criticism by a few Islamic intellectuals. The danger in such a Hegelian
interpretation of the modern Islamic world is generally seen in it being

unacceptable in Islamic societies because it is too elitist and does not properly take the real discourses on Islam into account. In order to reach the public and thereby gain influence, it would be necessary to adapt the way we speak about Islam to the social cultures. On the other hand, Islam is determined by political reality; thus, in order to have an influence over politics, it would be necessary to accept and use current ways of talking about Islam. This pragmatic solution is certainly the most prominent today. It is accepted that those in the public and political arena who propagate ideological categories that make Islam an all-encompassing solution, and do so in the most popularising way, are the ones who hold sway. The slogan 'Islam is the answer' *(al-islam huwa al-hall)* helps to formulate the categories which will determine the realisation of social development. The following are some of these categories:

- the symbolic use of the concept of Sharia (Islamic law)
- the realisation of society's ideals by reference to the early days of Islam
- the construction of the Koran as the 'pure Muhammadan tradition of the Prophet' *(al-sunnah al-nabawiyah al-muhammadiyah al-mutahharah)* – the extra-temporal Truth confirmed by the text
- valuing religion only when it is practised publicly, i.e. when religion is political.

The rhetorical dovetailing of such categories creates a new concept of 'Islam' which has adapted itself to the prevailing cultural conditions of certain societies in the Middle East. Here too, Islam remains a culture which determines a network of social relationships which is conveyed through communication, and as a result of which a certain amount of unity does exist. The network which expresses such an Islam unites those social groups which have been denied all participation in the decision-making process of society in the last few decades. Under one-party regimes and military dictatorships that had – not without purpose – created a sizeable bureaucratic apparatus, large sections of the population were functionally integrated into the state, although not socially or culturally. People working in these bureaucracies could in no way achieve a social position that equated their functional position. What remained was their own lack of tradition which characterised their life in the functional concrete ghettos. Equipped with no cultural or social infrastructure, they lived separate from any decision-making process.

A hallmark of all Islamic movements was therefore a desire to complement people's functional purpose with a corresponding political eminence. Social reality demands that functional existence in administrations, schools and universities must be given a new symbolic meaning, and this had to be taken into account ideologically. This can best be achieved when those affected can themselves identify with the functional context of their environment and try to express it culturally. Thus a school shall become an Islamic school, a university an Islamic university. The attribute 'Islamic' clearly expresses this claim to identity. While actual state authority over education is understood to be anonymous, by contrast the assumption of an Islamic symbolism personalises it. Through the Islamicisation of the social network a new line of communication is produced which appears to be highly symbolic. To this belong the new Islamic dress code as much as the specifically Islamic language, and public manifestations of the collective sense of belonging to the network which is seen as a community *(jama'h)*. In this process, the level of agreement secured by members of the community is important. It is most often limited to a few categories whose intellectual interpretation has just been discussed.

## On the History of Islamic Politics

Islamic politics in the widest sense of the term has a very clear civil character. It is a protest against a functional existence, and demands participation or, more radically, sovereign power over the state which determines functional existence. It is, then, about reclaiming sovereignty and history through Islamic citizens, who want thereby to remove the political division of society and state. It is for this reason that almost all Islamic intellectuals stress the concept of sovereignty *(hakimiyah)*, which is to be restored to the citizens.[16] The legitimacy of sovereignty is achieved by referring *hakimiyah* to God, who for his part appointed the citizen as his representative *(khalifah)*. The distinction between God as sovereign and citizens as his representatives is theoretically strictly adhered to by most Islamic intellectuals. What is meant by this is above all the enhancement of the status of the citizen (vis-à-vis the state), legitimised through the acquisition of the historic Islamic will which had determined man[kind] for political leadership.

Within public Islamic politics, there has been no agreement about the question of what constituted this sovereignty and what the consequences for the ordering of society and state would be. The debate about Islamic sovereignty had already stirred Islamic citizens in the eighteenth century. From the fundamental identity of God as 'Creator' (legislature), Ruler (executive) and Judge (judiciary), the sovereign rights of man were derived and an analogous identity of man was defined.[17] How ruling power was to be deployed in society remained open. In the nineteenth century, Islamic intellectuals stressed the principle of the separation of powers, although individual scholars such as the well-known Egyptian writer Rifa'a Rafi' al-Tahtawi (who died in 1873) wanted to subordinate the separation of powers to enlightened absolutism.[18]

After 1870, the colonial situation created completely new conditions in most Islamic countries: many Islamic citizens felt culturally separated from 'their' state. First, in certain areas of control such as law or education, there were attempts to reclaim sovereignty or to defend the existing sovereignty. After 1900, an Islamic macrocosm was created in which people tried to uphold their civil identity in the face of the colonial states. Here in the virtual space of Islam, they found it possible to articulate their civil identity even though their influence on real state power was minimal. A characteristic of this macrocosm was the reference to the wholeness of the Islamic community *(ummah)*, which Islamic intellectuals wanted to represent politically. In this they were able to practise the sovereignty which had been denied them in the colonial states.

The Islamic macrocosm which was realised in the so-called Congress movement had been constructed entirely along the lines of the civil traditions and the separation of powers: the assemblies as the place of (moral) legislation, the local representations as the organs of an executive and Islamic academia as the judiciary.[19] In the 1920s and 1930s, when Islamic groups (such as the Egyptian Muslim Brotherhood from about 1928) became politically active outside the Congress movement, Islamic intellectuals were forced to take up political positions within the real states, which could express the drifting apart of state and society. The more marked this process became, the more radically was political and cultural reintegration demanded. The degree of radicalness finally determined whether the civil principle of the separation of powers could still be upheld or not. In the 1930s, populist programmes which demanded the removal of the separation of powers in favour of an Islamic state could mobilise more supporters than civil-democratic programmes. In this specific form of fascism, Islam became an ideology of salvation, a 'movement' *(harakah)*, which promised individual supporters might, power and authority. The theoretical foundations of the Islamic right were – one could not expect otherwise – of low standard. It was not intellectual debates that were needed, but action and propaganda. It is only after the Second World War that the Islamic debate about state, society and power achieved the same level as it had at the beginning of the twentieth century. The failure of right-wing Islamic populism allowed Islamic intellectuals once more to take up the question about power and rule. A wide spectrum of political positions gradually emerged, ranging from anarchist programmes for action to socialist interpretations and bourgeois concepts, and right-wing radical and racist ideologies.

## An Islamic Citizenry

At the beginning of the 1970s Islamic groups made a great breakthrough. They defined themselves ever more clearly as the only real political representatives of the civil society and were gradually able to absorb other ideological lines of thought. Supported, among other sources, by Saudi Arabian oil money they created their own press which in turn further sharpened their image. The civil protest now directed itself against the separation of state and society, which was symbolically taken up by the formula 'The Separation of Religion and State'. Civil society's claim to integration in the state found an equally symbolic counterpart in the popular slogan 'Islam is the religion and the state' (*al-islam din wa-dawlah*).[20] Here, religion (*din*) stands for Islamic citizens' claims to sovereignty, which itself derives from Islamic dogma. Such a religious concept is very close to the American concept of a 'civil religion'.[21]

Reverting to the use of religion as a symbol has had two serious consequences for Islamic citizens: in the first place, it has prevented a critical recognition of civil society in countries in the Middle East by Western observers, who, for reasons mentioned above, did not believe a civil opposition within Islamic culture was possible. The West's failure to recognise Islamic citizenry as the avant-garde of any citizenry led Islamic intellectuals to speak ever more clearly against the West's international sovereignty, and to plead for cultural separation from the West.

Second, reverting to religion created a new religious discourse on Islam, which indeed made religion the determining ideological factor. Islamic faith became a part of the political programme even though faith and bourgeois rationality would appear to exclude each other. This new discourse reconstructed Islam as a religion, although religion now had a completely different meaning from that of, say, 300 years ago. Political realism now dominated religion. The symbolic framework of religion and even its transcendental references were subordinate to the citizens' interest in removing the separation from the state. The power of the word 'religion' now turned out to be a hindrance in two respects: first, it prevented recognition by the 'unreligious' West, and second Islamic groups were themselves victims of the power of religion. Since religion was considered an unchangeable fact of Islamic citizenry, the possibility of criticising it shifted to the background. Criticism as the most important constant of intellectual existence was subjected to an important self-limitation. As a result, Islamic politics were once again divided in two camps: that of society, which was to be subject to thorough criticism, and that of religion whose unalterable character had been established. The idealistic notion of Islamic politics as the executor of history once again became part of the religious identity.

The absence of religious criticism necessarily limits the efficacy of the Islamic citizenry.[22] It is not surprising, then, that the question of religious criticism was also posed afresh within the framework of the debate on modernity and authenticity. Islamic intellectuals such as the Moroccan Muhammad abid al-Jabiri or the French teacher and scholar of Islamic studies of Algerian-Berber extraction Muhammad Arkoun undertook the re-evaluation of religion within the framework of the French debate on postmodernism. They demanded dispensing with anachronistic criticism of religion in the tradition of the Enlightenment, and instead completely re-evaluating religion as a cultural discourse.[23] Thus, the discussion of Islam as a religion was brought in line with the new criticism of modernity.

The diversity of political, philosophical and religious-historical criticism by Islamic intellectuals on the condition of contemporary Islamic citizenry is impressive. It is, however, at the same time depressing to see that this criticism has hardly penetrated into the real political debate. More than ever before, the Islamic public is dominated by political groups that have no interest in a criticism of the Islamic bourgeois identity, because they have to interpret all criticism as loss of power. The kind of public constituted by these Islamic groups is not only financially dependent on powerful states such as Saudi Arabia or Iran and therefore prone to censorship, it also exercises a determining influence on Islamic discourse. Here Islam appears to be flat, devoid of any intellectual sophistication and dogmatised. The strength of such a public also stems from the fact that the West's failure to recognise the Islamic citizenry has strengthened the self-affirmation of Islamic intellectuals, which often leads to any nominal analogy with the West having to be eradicated, whether in the area of democracy, human rights, power sharing or modernity itself. The failure of Western policies and the West's readiness to recognise Islamic citizenry peaked during the Gulf War, when scores of Islamic intellectuals went over to populist Islamic positions and in so doing even gave up the building blocks of their own intellectual identity such as criticism and ethics.

Whether or not Islamic intellectuals will be able to assert themselves again as a critical authority in society is largely dependent on the extent to which an Islamic citizenry which manifests itself in entirely heterogeneous Islamic civil movements will be recognised by the Western press. The West's tendency to reduce Islamic intellectual culture to 'fundamentalism' or to identify it with anachronistic references to early Islam threaten to suffocate the independence of intellectual criticism in Islamic societies.

## Notes

1   This conviction is also represented in the new literature of Islamic studies and the social sciences. Representative for many titles are: A. Hourani, *Arabic Thought in the Liberal Age, 1798–1939*, London: Cambridge University Press, 1962 (cf. however, Hourani's reassessment in the foreword to the second edition (New York, 1983)) and B. Tibi, *Die Krise des modernen Islam*, Frankfurt am Main: Suhrkamp Publ., 1981.

2   Widely differing elaborating interpretations are derived from this basic position. They range from the description of Islamic culture as an irrational counterpart to modernism, to interpretations of Islamic culture as a preindustrial one which 'has reached a state of crisis' as a result of not coping with Westernisation.

3   The re-evaluation of the history and culture of the Far East is very different. See, for example Du-Yol Song, 'Asien zwischen Moderne und ihren Kritikern', *Peripherie*, 32 1988, pp. 7–21 and the literature quoted therein.

4   The Arabic word for intellectual *mufakkirun* cannot, however, be a borrowing from the West, as it is older than the 'European' word *'intellectuel'*. The first instance of the word *mufakkirun* dates from the year 1881, whereas that of the French word *intellectuel* (as a noun) from the year 1898. On the latter, see D. Bering, *Die Intellektuellen. Geschichte eines Schimpfwortes*, Frankfurt am Main: Suhrkamp Publ., 1982. Arabic designations which describe a separate intellectual Islamic culture can be traced well back into the eighteenth century. The beginning of a specific Islamic intellectual culture can be conservatively dated to the middle of the eighteenth century. See also Note 13.

5   The other word for the modern age, *mu'asarah* appears, according
    to a first and cautious interpretation, to be used more commonly
    in an Egyptian-Syrian context. While *mu'asarah* can be understood
    as a purely temporal term ('the contemporary'), *hadathah* often
    has a qualitative aspect of meaning which stems from the old
    philosophical tradition, carrying with it the notion of separation
    from the old and the pre-eminence of the new (*hadith*) over the
    old (*qadim*). A concise overview of individual definitions can be
    found in G. Hoffman's '"al-turath" und "al-mu'asarah" in der
    Diskussion arabischer Intellektueller der Gegenwart', in W.
    Reuschel (ed.), *Orientalistische Philologie und Arabische Linguistik*,
    AAL Sonderheft 2, Berlin, 1990, pp. 50-4.
6   B. Tibi's essay in the new edition of his book *Die Krise des
    modernen Islam*, Frankfurt am Main: Suhrkamp Publ., 1991, is a
    worthwhile example on this subject.
7   Examples are H. Djait, *Europe and Islam. Cultures and Modernity*,
    Berkeley, University of California Press, 1985, A. Laroui, *L'Idéologie
    arabe contemporaine*, Paris, 1967, and his *Islam et modernité*, Paris,
    1987. See also L. Binder, *Islamic Liberalism. A Critique of Devel-
    opment Ideologies*, Chicago, 1988, p. 317ff.
8   This basis can also be ethnic, according to the political standpoint;
    thus for example, it can refer to either 'Arabdom' or 'Berberdom'.
9   At the beginning of the twentieth century this was how Christian
    Arab intellectuals also saw it, for example cf. G. Zaidan, *ta'rikh
    al-tamaddun al-islami*, I-V, Cairo, 2nd edn 1914–19, 3rd edn
    1921–2.
10  One of the most important conferences on the theme took place
    in Cairo from 24 to 27 September 1984, see *Markaz dirasat al-
    wahda al-'arabiyah, al-turath wa-tahaddiyat al-'asr fi al-watan
    al-'arabi. al-asalah wa-al-mu'asarah*, Beirut, 1985.
11  Some Islamic intellectuals try to qualify the axiom of the validity
    of early Islam; see for example, Seyyed Hossein Nasr, *Traditional
    Islam in the Modern World*, London and New York: Kegan Paul
    International, 1987. Nasr taught philosophy from 1958–1979 at
    Tehran University and is now Professor of Islamic Studies at
    George Washington University.
12  As for example, R. Peters, 'Erneuerungsbewegungen im Islam vom
    18. bis 20. Jahrhundert und die Rolle des Islams in der neueren
    Geschichte: Antikolonialismus und Nationalismus', in W. Ende
    and U. Steinbach (eds), *Der Islam der Gegenwart*, Munich:
    Kohlhammer Publ., 1984, pp. 91–131, especially p. 105ff.

13  The Arabic word *mufakkirun* for 'intellectual' tends to be used
    in a political Islamic context today. In non-Islamic areas the
    description *muthaqqafun* (really 'educated') is more commonly
    used.

14  *al-yawm akmaltu lakum dinakum* (Koran 5/3). It goes on: 'and I
    have completed my blessing upon you, and I have approved Islam
    for your religion', trans. Arthur J. Arberry, *The Koran Interpreted*,
    London and New York: George Allen & Unwin Ltd, 1955.

15  The special structural closeness of Islam to modernity is also
    recognised by E. Gellner, *Muslim Societies*, 2nd edn, Cambridge:
    Cambridge University Press 1983, p. 7. See also F. Büttner,
    'Zwischen Politisierung und Säkularisierung – Möglichkeiten
    und Grenzen einer islamischen Integration der Gesellschaft', in
    E. Forndran (ed.), *Religion und Politik in einer säkularisierten Welt*,
    Baden-Baden, 1991, pp. 137–67.

16  The concept of *hakimiyah* which is so popular today comes from
    Turkish-Ottoman political language of the nineteenth
    (eighteenth?) century and in the first instance very generally
    describes sovereignty within a state. An etymological history of
    this meaning does not as yet exist. For example, there is no
    reference to this term in A. Ayalon, *Language and Political change
    in the Arab Middle East. The Evolution of Modern Arabic Political
    Discourse*, Oxford: Oxford University Press, 1987.

17  On this see R. Schulze, 'Das islamische 18. Jahrhundert. Versuch
    einer historiographischen Kritik', *Die Welt des Islams*, 30, 1990,
    pp. 140–59.

18  Especially in his work *manahij al-albab al-misriyah fi mabahij al-
    adab al-'asriyah*, Bulaq/Cairo, 1286/1869. Cf. G. Delanoue,
    *Moralistes et politiques musulmans dans l'Égypte du XIXe siècle
    (1798–1882)*, Cairo, 1982, p. 462ff.

19  See M. Kramer, *Islam Assembled. The Advent of Muslim Congresses*,
    New York, 1986; J. M. Landau, *The Politics of Pan-Islam. Ideology
    and Organization*, Oxford: Oxford University Press, 1990; R.
    Schulze, *Islamischer Internationalismus im 20. Jahrhundert*, Leiden,
    1990.

20  It appears highly significant to me that this set phrase is a good
    150 years old. On the political and ideological background of
    such symbolic interpretations, see for example R. Schulze, 'Islam
    und Herrschaft. Zur politischen Instrumentalisierung einer
    Religion', in M. Lüders (ed.), *Der Islam im Aufbruch? Perspektive
    der arabischen Welt*, Munich: Piper Publ., 1992, pp. 94–129.

21   Raised by the American sociologist R. N. Bellah in 1967; see R. Döbert, '"Zivilreligion". Ein religiöses Nichts religionstheoretisch betrachtet', *Kursbuch 93*, 1988, pp. 67–84, and other literature therein.

22   This was above all emphasized by the Syrian philosopher Sadiq al-Azm.

23   Cf. M. abid al-Jabiri, *nahnu wa-l-turath – qira'ah mu'asirah fi turathinah al-falsafi*, Beirut/Casablanca, 1985; M. Arkoun, 'Islam und Weltlichkeit', *Gewissen und Freiheit*, 36, 1991[1], pp. 32–57.

# 4

# 'Islam is in Danger': Authority, Rushdie and the Struggle for the Migrant Soul

*Fred Halliday*

It has not required recent rhetorical excesses of Islamists or anti-Muslim demagogues to remind us of the complex and long-standing tension between the Islamic world and a predominantly Christian and now secular Europe. One can begin with the geographical and, by derivation, strategic reality that it is the Islamic peoples who constitute the outer boundary of Europe, forming a vast semi-circle that abuts on to the lands to its south and east, from Ceuta and Melilla on the Straits of Gibraltar to the Caucasus and the Tatar region of Russia. This is the part of the colonial Third World that is Europe's neighbour. The three great earlier periods of conflict between the Islamic and non-Islamic West remain etched in history – the rise of Islam in the late seventh century which brought its armies into Sicily and well into France, the medieval wars of the Crusaders that ended only when the Ottomans were halted, in the seventeenth century, at Vienna, and a third, beginning in the late eighteenth century, when European states subjugated the Muslim world to their political and economic domination.

A fourth, as yet unresolved, epoch of Islamic interaction with Europe appears to have begun in the aftermath of the Second World War, and especially since the early 1970s. As with the three earlier ages of conflict it is primarily about power – the power of states, the power to dictate practices and culture, and to control resources. Beliefs enter into it, but they are intertwined with other, recognisably secular and material, concerns. One dimension of this new conflict is at the international level: the rise, in response to centuries of invasion and occupation, of nationalisms within Islamic countries that are, to a greater or lesser extent, phrased in religious terms, ranging from the mildly Islamic nationalism of a Nasser to the Islamist populism of Khomeini; the increased prominence of the oil-producing states, who have used their money in part to promote Islamic practices

71

and movements that are sympathetic to them, as dynasties and states. Within these countries, the prominence of religion in political movements has been assisted by two factors: the association of secularism with an authoritarian modernisation from above in a range of countries, such that populist revolt assumes a more religious hue (Iran, Afghanistan, Turkey, Egypt, Algeria); and the conflict of Islamic peoples with states and communities of other faiths (Hinduism, Judaism, as well as Christianity) against which religious anger is directed. Islamic ideas have, therefore, become part of the conflict between one group of Third World states and peoples and their regional and great-power opponents.

This conflict is evident not only in relations between states, but also in the incidence of communal conflicts: for contemporary and modern rather than 'traditional' reasons, conflict within states is now rife along the historic frontiers of the Islamic and Christian worlds – in Kosovo, Cyprus, Lebanon, Egypt, the Caucasus. Here forms of tolerance or relative peace have, as a result of new nationalist and social tensions, been overtaken by intensified hatreds. We can expect to hear a lot more about this, not least from the former Soviet Union, where, despite decades of 'internationalist' propaganda from the top, few lessons appear to have been learnt, and every small ethnic group is now vaunting its 'history' and grievances. Although reflecting a comparatively recent demographic change, through Jewish immigration since the 1870s, the Palestine issue has acquired a similar communal character, decked out with much supposedly legitimating history, while on the other side of the Islamic world there are other Muslim/non-Muslim tensions aflame, from Assam to southern Sudan.

This fourth epoch of conflict has, however, received sustenance from another development, namely the growth within the developed world itself of Islamic communities which now represent a significant force in many countries. Conversion to Islam has not been a significant trend, except in the United States: in Europe a Roger Garaudy – the former French communist now a Muslim convert – and the occasional Sufi do not constitute a mass shift. The main reason for the surge in Islamic communities has been migration: in Britain, France, Germany and numerous other countries – Holland, Switzerland, Sweden – there are now established Islamic communities born of this recent migration. Precise figures are impossible to come by, but the broad picture based on rough indicators is as follows: in Britain there are 750,000–1 million Muslims; in France, there are over 3 million; in Germany, the figure is believed to be around 1.75 million. The total for Western Europe is over 6 million.[1]

For all the differences of origin and country of residence, these communities evince some common characteristics. First, while the migration itself took place overwhelmingly in the 1950s and 1960s, before recession and immigration controls sealed it off, it was in the 1970s and 1980s that there occurred a remarkable surge in religiosity, in the public demonstration of Islamic faith. This is evident in the numbers of mosques: there are over 1,000 of these in France, and the number in Britain rose from fifty-one in 1970 to 329 in 1985, the great majority in converted houses or flats. The trend is equally evident in the activities of Islamic associations and community groupings, hundreds of which exist in each major state. This increase in religious visibility among immigrants has also led to campaigns on issues of special importance for believers in Islam: the availability of halal meat, the provision of places of worship, respect for Islamic practices in education, the clothing and segregation of Islamic women.

Many of these campaigns reflect alarm about the maintenance of control within the community, more than about the threat from a non-Islamic world without: in every country Islamic leaders express concern about the degree to which the second-generation immigrants, by now up to half the total, will continue to respect the faith. In Paris and Lyon, as in Birmingham and Bradford, the young, as distinct from the very young, are not proportionately present in the mosque. The increased religiosity of the 1970s and 1980s may go some way to reversing this, but it is too early to say. Yet some factors common to different West European countries have encouraged increased religious identification: the closing of frontiers to further immigration has reduced the degree of circulation of migrants and has therefore made it clear that those now resident are going to stay; the rise of racist attacks on Muslims – evident not only in 'Paki-bashing' in Britain but in the rise of Le Pen in France and far-right activities in Germany – has forced many in the second generation to qualify hopes for full integration; the money and encouragement of Islamic states have also played their role, as have certain international events, such as the Iranian revolution, the attacks on Libya, the Palestinian intifada and Bosnia.

If these substantial Islamic communities share common concerns, they are also marked by enormous differences. This makes it impossible to form any general picture or 'sociology' of West European Muslims. First of all, Islam is a centrifugal religion: it has no even putative centre – the caliphate was abolished by Atatürk in 1924 and had long since ceased to act as an authority even for Sunni Muslims – and this is reflected in the variety of sects and orientations that are present within the communities. Unlike many Christian groupings it is impossible to identify a centre of authority or leadership. This fragmentation within Islam as such is compounded by the religious changes that occur in emigration: while it is safe to assume that many migrants retain the beliefs of their place of origin, there is much adoption of Islamic ideas from other sources, ones to which they have been exposed only in exile. Thus Yemeni migrants in Britain in the 1930s and 1940s were organized by a religious sect, the Alawiyya, based in Algeria.[2] Among French Muslims of North African origin there has in recent years been considerable support for Jama'at al-Tabligh, the Society of Propagation, a proselytising grouping founded in India in 1927 whose European headquarters is in Britain. The experience of migration both confirms a desire to assert or reassert certain traditional values and exposes the migrant to new ones. The parallel with communist recruitment of migrants is striking: indeed in France many Arabs and Turks now live in former strongholds of the French Communist Party (PCF). It is not for nothing that the most prominent centre of the autonomous 'French' Muslims is *la mosquée de Stalingrad*, and that its worshippers live in the rue Youri Gagarin and the avenue Maurice Thorez.

To these religious differences are added those of a national, linguistic and political character. The 'Muslims' of Western Europe, who appear homogeneous to the non-Islamic world and to the, usually self-appointed, official representatives of Islam, also come from a variety of national backgrounds: in Britain Pakistanis, Bengalis and Indians, but also Turkish Cypriots and a variety of Arabs; in Germany, Turks and Yugoslavs; in France, Algerians, Moroccans, Tunisians, Senegalese, Mauritanians, Turks. Even these 'national' labels conceal local and linguistic divisions – between Pathans, Punjabis and Gujeratis, between Kurds and Turks, between Algerian Arabs and Kabyles, let alone between different kinds of Arab. If the countries of origin differ, so too do the countries of reception: in Britain, Commonwealth immigrants were automatically granted the vote, something denied in France and Germany; on the other hand, the French government has, from the mid-1970s onwards, provided special housing for immigrants, and encouraged the building of places of worship in immigrant estates. Some French firms provide these at the place of work. In Britain such provision for immigrant religious needs is almost inconceivable: here much energy has been expended in conflict over an especially British issue, school uniforms.

The variety of currents and organisations within the Islamic communities of Western Europe is, moreover, compounded by the fissiparous impact of Islamic states, many of which have tried to influence the communities abroad with financial and other induce-ments. At one level this takes the form of funding mosques and publications, where religious duty and state interest coincide: Saudi Arabia has specialised in this, and through the Islamic World League in Mecca operates its own transnational organisation. Since 1979 the Islamic Republic of Iran has also sought to build up a following in this way, albeit with fewer resources: the Ayatollah's Rushdie campaign was, in part, designed to strengthen his claim to be the leader of *all* Muslims. Other states use religious links as a way of maintaining administrative, and coercive, control over those from their own countries: visas, funds, channelling of remittances, access to buildings all help to keep the migrants in line. Others still try to use the Islamic communities as a way of extending what are basically secular political interests; Libya and Iraq, for example, have given money for this purpose, as an extension of inter-Arab conflict. Beyond the influence of states, Islamic parties in the home countries have built up networks abroad. An obvious case is that of the Jama'at-i-Islam of Pakistan, a right-wing group with Saudi connections that has strong support among Muslims in Britain: it organises Pakistanis in Britain in support of campaigns both there and in Pakistan.[3] One final twist to this tale of fragmentation is that of the competition between Arabs and non-Arabs for primacy within Islam. The Turkish imams in France consider that their people understand more of the Koran than the Arabs,[4] and Gaddafi has denounced non-Arab influences, including the Tabligh, within Islam. It can be noted that there is more than a trace of this ancient cultural and religious rivalry in *The Satanic Verses*, and in the response to it.

Despite these evident diversities, the myth, perpetuated by Muslims and non-Muslims alike, is that this 'Islam' and the Islamic commu-nities represent one community, one *ummah*. This has never been true of the Islamic world, and is certainly not true of the Muslims of Western Europe. The variety and fluidity under the apparently universal cover of Islam touches on a recurrent aspect of all study of 'Islamic' society, whether in Western Europe or in the relevant Third World countries, namely how far the very designation 'Islam' provides a key to understanding how such groups behave in the social and political arenas. For all its claims to prescribe for social and individual as well as political behaviour, the variety of practices in Islamic countries suggests that 'Islam' as such cannot explain how Muslims behave, or how they might/ought to behave. Other factors outside 'Islam' must be invoked. The resort to an all-explanatory 'Islam' is therefore circular. Moreover, these 'Muslims', as much as the rest of us, have multiple identities, the relative balance and character of which change over time. It is one of the intriguing but elusive challenges of any analysis of these 'Muslims' to disentangle and chart the relation between these different identities. The study of Islamic communities cannot be based on a 'sociology of religion' alone; it must, rather, involve a sociology of how religion interacts with other ethnic, cultural and political forces.

To take the example of one long-standing Arab community in Britain: in the eight decades since they have been resident in Britain, the Yemenis, a community of at most 15,000, have been identified by a variety of terms as Lascars, negroes, blacks, Asians, Arabs, Yemenis, Muslims, Pakistanis; to which must be added their own regional variations – North or South Yemeni, Shafei or Zeidi Muslim, alignment of one or other faction with their respective regime in Sana'a and Aden, and the tribal and regional variations, Dhali'i, Yafi'i, Maqbani, Shamiri and so on.[5] In much discussion of Western Europe, this problem recurs.[6] Such usage does not sufficiently address the question of how far the separateness and distinctness of Muslims in France is a matter of their being Muslims, or of their being Arabs, or Algerians, or identifying with some subdivision. There is very little room in such a polarity for discussion of the place of an Arab, or Algerian, identity in the life of these people and of how religious activities, publications, meeting-places interact with the political. Equally, comparative studies of West European Muslims tend to treat their subject matter in too restrictedly religious a manner. Yet as is evident from the mosques of Birmingham, attendance at these breaks down almost completely along national and regional lines: proclaiming belief in one God, Pathans, Punjabis, 'Campbellpuris', Azad Kashmiris, Bengalis, Yemenis, Gujeratis go their separate ways to prayer.[7]

Much of the discussion of West European Muslims focuses on issues of identity in a non-Islamic world, on questions of assimilation versus separateness, and on the distinction between 'insertion', that is finding a recognised but distinct place, and 'integration'.[8] There is no doubt that both kinds of process are at work. Many second-generation citizens from Muslim backgrounds mix with and share the values of their generation in West European society, and come to be critical of the national and religious backgrounds they come from: in France there are the second-generation North African writers, the *beurs* (slang for French-born Arab), in Britain we have Hanif Kureishi's *My Beautiful Laundrette*. Now that the doors of immigration have closed, it is harder to go back. At the same time the forces in favour of a negotiated 'insertion' have also gained ground: some through the widespread rise in religiosity in the 1970s, some through the exertions of Islamic states and organizations like the Tabligh. Islamic community and national organisations are now stronger and more vocal than ever before: in France they are a political force just as, increasingly, they are in Britain. The 1987 manifesto, *The Muslim Vote*, signed by twenty-four Islamic associations, sought to lay out a set of demands for Muslims in Britain, pertaining above all to education – clothing, food, single-sex teaching, avoidance of dancing, mixed bathing and sex education. In France and Britain policies designed to alter the educational system on general grounds have provided occasion for Muslim parents to voice special concerns.

What this suggests above all is that for all their assertiveness the Muslim communities in Western Europe feel themselves to be under threat: it is the fear of loss of control that animates their activities. Here, of course, their concern has been shared by many of the most vocal leaders of the Islamic world, including Khomeini. The Ayatollah was not particularly preoccupied with spreading the word of Islam, about conversion, or externally directed jihad. His rallying cry, before and after coming to power, was 'Islam is in danger'. Aggressive and aggrieved as it may be, it is a defensive call, one that found a special echo among Islamic leaders in Western Europe. It is this context, of erosion real or imagined, that underlay the reaction to *The Satanic Verses*. The fictionalised account of early Islam is, in itself, regarded by many Muslims as unacceptable, but this is equally a book about the Islamic experience in a West European country, in this case Britain.[9] It was, indeed, said of Salman Rushdie some years ago that after writing one book about India (*Midnight's Children*) and one about Pakistan (*Shame*), he would now write one about Britain. The book about Britain then appeared and, after the initial outrage on the part of Islamic officials, it was, appropriately, the turn of British ministers to denounce its anti-racist and satirical view of the United Kingdom, not least its reflections on the police.

The exploration of Rushdie's novel speaks for part of the migrant experience in that it turns a critical face both ways, towards the country of origin and its traditions and towards the country of reception. The challenge, the alienation and the 'offence' are two-sided. It is not casual that at one point Rushdie links the migrant to the blasphemer, since both act a part, both run the risk of causing offence. But Rushdie's challenge to the Islamic world, beyond a Rabelaisian account of early Islam, is to have broken away: Khomeini has accused him of *kufr–i jahani*, 'world blasphemy', but the term *kufr* and its adjective *kafir* contain several meanings: not only atheism and blasphemy, but also apostasy.[10] It is this latter charge that is the most serious, since, in writing as he did, of Muhammad, of doubt, of the profane masquerading as the religious, Rushdie represents a challenge within the faith that the embattled religious leaders, in Bradford and in Tehran, could not accept.

There is certainly a strictly religious foundation for such anathemas against those charged with 'blasphemy', in Islam as there is in Christianity and Judaism: Muhammad ordered the murder of Asma bint Marwan, a woman poet who criticised him, just as in the Bible Leviticus 24 enjoins us to stone all such offenders. But the question of why such injunctions from another age have been invoked here and now can only be answered by reference to current social and political concerns: all the great victims of blasphemy charges (Socrates, Christ, Galileo, Spinoza) were also charged with sedition. It is in such political concerns that the roots of the campaign around *The Satanic Verses* can be comprehended: Islam is 'in danger', and it is seen to be under threat not so much from without, something that has always been the case, as from loss of belief and of submission within.

What appears, therefore, to be a conflict between Islam and the external, non-Islamic world is above all a reflection of a conflict within the Islamic world. The greatest consequence of the Iranian revolution has been to divide the Muslim world more grievously than ever before, and the same may well turn out to be the case with the response to *The Satanic Verses*. The reaction of Tunisian fundamentalists may be indicative in this regard: they are saying that people should stop worrying about 'the British Rushdie' and instead concentrate energies on the 'Rushdies' among their own people, by which they mean the secularisers and those proclaiming the equality of men and women.

There will not be, indeed there cannot be, any easy resolution of the problems posed by the relations between the Islamic and Western worlds or by the issues raised through the activities of Islamic religious groups in Western Europe. One reason is that, however much talk there is of dialogue and 'understanding', very different principles are involved – not just of food or clothing, but of authority, law, gender relations, power. Another is that the very variety and fragmentation of what are regarded as 'Muslim' communities make any resolution more difficult. But at this point a distinction becomes relevant that pertains not just to Islam, but to all the major religions: Christianity, Judaism, Hinduism, Buddhism. That distinction is between a religion that respects certain general principles of contemporary democratic life, including a public secularism and related concepts of tolerance, and one that does not.

It is this theme which a number of critical voices from Muslim countries have themselves addressed in powerful critiques of the intellectual assumptions of most Islamic thought.[11] They do not argue that Islam is incapable of adjusting to the modern world, but they do show, without flinching and on the basis of their own experiences, just how introverted, incoherent and self-defeating most Islamic political thinking to date has been. They have some especially telling observations to make about the meandering rhetoric of Islamic politicians, and the failure to comprehend what modern industrial society involves. Equally they are clear about the solution, remote as it may be: the Islamic world has to adopt a critical and rational view of its own past, texts and religious doctrines, and has to accept the central values of Western society, namely secularism, rationality and genuine tolerance of divergent beliefs. They contend that neither the traditionalists nor the Islamic modernists have broken with the doctrinal constraints that inhibit them. There is more than a little in the furore over *The Satanic Verses*, and the impasse of the Iranian revolution from which Khomeini's diversionary use of it stemmed, to confirm this analysis.

There is also much in the Western response to the rise of Islamic fundamentalists that is itself open to question: the very Western governments that were outraged at Khomeini's condemnation of Rushdie armed people of very similar hue in Afghanistan; the issue of fundamentalism is one that runs within all the major religions, not between Islam and the rest; those who rightly dislike what Iran is trying to do in the international arena, and are puzzled by its nationalist fervour, forget too easily what the British have done, during the course of this century, to Iran – invading it on two occasions, in collusion with their wartime ally, Russia, and conspiring with the United States in the early 1950s to oust and murder members of its elected government. But to recognize these complexities is not to deny the great importance of the issues posed in the clash between a Khomeinite view of the world and that of secular democracy. The Ayatollah and his supporters had little interest in dialogue, as they have shown in over fifteen years of theocratic dictatorship.

In the end, the outcome of this conflict will be determined more by what happens within the Islamic world than by relations between the Islamic countries and the states outside. It is here, perhaps, that the Muslim communities of Western Europe may assume a special importance, containing as they do people more informed about the non-Muslim world than those living in Islamic lands and who, for all the attempts to prevent their changing, are adapting to and engaging with the secular world around them. If there is to be any hope of an intellectual and cultural breakthrough within the Islamic world, one that goes beyond the minority of brave, if at times imprudent, writers and thinkers who have always challenged doctrinal powers, then it may well come from the *ummah* in exile: that, of course, is precisely what calls to order, on Rushdie, the position of women or education, have been designed to forestall.

## Notes

An earlier version of this article was published in The Times Literary Supplement, 14–20 April 1989.

1   Gilles Kepel, *Les Banlieues de l'Islam: Naissance d'une Religion en France,* Paris: Seuil, 1989; Tomas Gerholm and Yngve Georg Lithman (eds), *The New Islamic Presence in Western Europe,* London: Mansell, 1988; and Jorgen Nielsen, *Muslims in Western Europe,* Edinburgh: Edinburgh University Press, 1992.

2   See Fred Halliday, *Arabs in Exile. Yemeni Communities in Urban Britain,* London: I. B. Tauris, 1992.

3   John Rex in his essay on Birmingham in Gerholm and Lithman, *The New Islamic Presence.*

4   Kepel, *Les Banlieues de l'Islam.*

5   Halliday, *Arabs in Exile.*

6   Kepel appears to work with a dichotomy 'French/Muslim', as if the two were alternatives.

7   Daniele Joly in Gerholm and Lithman, *The New Islamic Presence.*

8   Kepel, *Les Banlieues de l'Islam.*

9   Malise Ruthven, *A Satanic Affair,* London: Chatto & Windus, 1990; Lisa Appignanesi and Sara Maitland (eds), *The Rushdie File,* London: Fourth Estate, 1989.

10   There is no exact Muslim equivalent to the Christian concept of blasphemy, the term used in the Greek New Testament to describe the charge on which Christ, who claimed he was the King of the Jews, was tried and executed – from the Greek *blapto,* to harm, and *pheme,* speech. The Koranic terms *kufr, shirk* (literally 'sharing' or denying the oneness of God) and *ilhad* (literally 'digression', hence 'apostasy') are used interchangeably to cover atheism (i.e. the denial of divine beings in general), apostasy (i.e. rejection of one's particular religion), heresy (i.e. the assertion of beliefs contrary to the orthodox faith) and insult to the divine being (this latter being the core meaning of the Western term 'blasphemy'). Note, however, that in Islamic tradition all pertain to the Muslim's attitude to Allah, not to the Prophet, the latter being only a human being, in contrast to the Christian concept

of Jesus as both man and God. However, in South Asian Islam in particular, the figure of the Prophet is invested with a special sanctity and alleged insults to him are thus treated as forms of *kufr* or whatever.

11  Bassam Tibi, *The Crisis of Modern Islam: A Preindustrial Culture in the Scientific-Technological Age*, translated by Judith von Sivers, Salt Lake City: University of Utah Press, 1989; and Darius Shayegan, *Cultural Schizophrenia: Islamic Societies Confronting the West*, London: Saqi Books, 1992.

# 5

# Islam and Politics in the Middle East

*Azmy Bishara*

Political religion is, paradoxically, the outcome of a secular process culminating in the separation of church and state. Religion, as Western social sciences recognise, is a social phenomenon and fills a social role. The secularisation model presupposes that religion may be apolitical. This may be true in concept or even in some historical forms of religiosity, but religiosity in most of its specific forms has a political meaning and function, and theology, the mediation between the divine word and secular power, is fraught with politics. Restricting religion to the private domain contradicts the essence of religion, and the tension that accompanies the secularisation processes is rooted in this contradiction.[1]

The secularisation of culture (or science, or law, or politics) means the elimination of religion from the domain of culture and the transformation of that domain to one which is neutral (and no longer competent) in religious matters. The religious dimension that was formerly an integral part of a social phenomenon such as culture or law is now relegated to the province of the individual.

Pure secularisation exists only as a theoretical model. Nowhere today is the state wholly neutral in matters of religion, nor are religious establishments at all neutral when it comes to political affairs. When religion has been displaced from social domains to the exclusive province of the individual, it attempts to intrude back into society. Secular domains, moreover, contain remnants of the holy, which is the main component of religion. A Hegelian would be tempted to see political religious movements as a resecularisation of religion, and to explain political movements that sanctify secular values as agents of the same tension, i.e. as social representatives of tension in the concept of religion.

In any description of, say, the 'religion of reason' of the French Revolution, the category of religion functions only as analogy, more than an illustrative metaphor but short of the phenomenon chosen for comparison. In reality radical nationalist or socialist movements which promote political myths to cult status, have failed, as a matter of historical record, to become new religions. The politicisation of religion takes place at the point when religion reinfiltrates politics. In this sense, what is nowadays called 'fundamentalism' is nothing but political religion. (Political movements can take on a religious hue – heavy use of myth, cults of land and power, for example – but none of this alters the secular context or domain in which these processes take place. In these cases we are speaking of politics with religious attributes, (sacralised politics), not of political religion (secularised politics).

The theological transformations of religion into ideology – into an ordered system of ideas and values that serves as a means of social cohesion and acts to promote secular power – does not contradict the process of secularisation. Indeed, the germ of separation between church and state is apparent in the very use of religion as an ideology. 'When religion has lost its affinity with the transcendental', wrote Ernst Cassirer (1955: 73), 'the process of secularisation has reached its culmination.'

In the wake of the secularisation process, there will emerge religious movements that intrude back into the political domain, utilising symbols that clash with the tendency to sanctify secular nationalist (or socialist) symbols.[2] Placing religion beyond the political, outside the stream of national or otherwise collective experience, paves the way for viewing religion as a stable, unchanging phenomenon (Gilsenan 1988: 177). The removal of religion from the collective domain further implies the possibility of its transformation into something pure, reliable and intimate, something capable of providing shelter in an uncertain world while in theory and/or ideology it renders feasible the ahistorical view of an transhistorical religious essence, a view shared by Orientalists and Islamists alike, especially with regard to the political doctrines supposedly essential for and typical of Islam.

No less worrying is the ahistorical approach to 'political Islam' in many quasi-historical, quasi-journalistic books. Rigid dogmas have coalesced even in the writings of several Orientalists, such as that Islam differs from the other monotheistic religions in that it lays down a comprehensive system of rules of conduct arranging every aspect of social life, equivalent to rules of worship that organise the individual's relationship to the transcendental. Thus, for example, one scholar writes that 'Islamism ... was always present under the surface'. This, of course, is because Islam is 'different' in that it invariably yokes religion to the state and presumes to a universalist ordering of human and social life (Ghaussy 1989: 83–4).[3]

Such attitudes and statements are also typical of the literature generated by the contemporary Islamic political movements themselves. There is hardly any group or subgroup affiliated with political Islam that does not claim to be the continuation of the 'pure' Islam of the Prophet Muhammad, as if the Prophet were the leader of some modern religious political party. There is hardly a single Islamist spokesperson who does not argue that Islam is 'different' and 'special', in that it provides an entire system of social regulations. Opponents of Orientalism in the West and liberal Islamic thinkers and secular Muslims in the East all argue, by contrast, that 'fundamentalism' and Islam are not identical, and political Islam must be viewed in its social and historical context. In view of the stubborn refusal of Orientalists and Islamist movements alike to see Islam in historical perspective, Schulze (1988: 144) concludes that this is because such a historical perspective would adversely affect the ideology and self-consciousness of both.

## From Fundamentalism to Political Religion

The term 'fundamentalist' was first used with reference to a group of US Protestant churches which arose in the 1920s out of millenarian movements that had sprung up in that country nearly a century earlier, in the 1830s. 'A motley group of theologically conservative communities, which emphasize total and even literal inspiration from the Holy Scriptures and their absolute authority in matters of faith and works', was how the *Encyclopaedia Britannica* (1973–4: VII, 777) described them. The term eventually came to be used for all religious movements that seek to return to 'fundamentals', and to any movement seeking political power for the purpose of governing according to religious values.

In contemporary usage, even secular movements or factions have called themselves fundamentalist; the Greens in Germany, for instance, divide themselves into the Fundis and the Realos. The term is now deployed to describe so many phenomena – in different societies and different historical phases – that it no longer explains anything at all. In a recent collection of essays, editor Thomas Meyer (1989: 15) defines fundamentalism as a rejection of enlightenment and modernisation. He further asserts that fundamentalism and 'the flight from modernism' are universal phenomena. Here the term has been applied to an enormous array of quite diverse phenomena, such as romanticism, political religion, religious conservatism, and virtually any manifestation politics with religious overtones.

In fact, political-religious movements are modern movements. They should not be seen as mere reactions to modernism, but as a cultural and social product that is itself modern or a modern reactionariness. Political religion, moreover, should not be confused with romantic aspirations to restore a lost harmony between the individual and society or between society and nature, a harmony destroyed by the processes of individualisation and capitalist industrialisation. Political religion should not be confused with popular or folk religion.

Moreover, within 'fundamentalism' we can detect at least two main political-religious trends on the theoretical level, each claiming various forms in reality:[4] (a) reformist trends which envisage a return to 'fundamentals' as the only way to adjust religion to modernity after undergoing a necessary process of purification from the religious myths and popular beliefs, practices and traditions. A specific example would be the Islamic reform movements in the nineteenth century, which made a case for the reunification of 'Islam' and politics, i.e. world affairs, after restoring fundamentals, as the only possible way to reform both world and religion; (b) political-religious movements and ideologies calling for a return to 'fundamentals' as a reaction to modernity and against change and reform. In contradiction to their alleged aims, these movements bring about a change in religion, modernising it in a certain sense: a fact that makes nonsense of their claims to authenticity.

After establishing the difference between political religion in its different forms and popular religiosities, we should look for the conditions that bring about the conjunction of political religion, usually a doctrinaire elitist phenomenon, and folk religion: an encounter that often imperils the stability of political systems in countries experiencing the social dislocations that accompany 'modernisation'. Such an encounter is not inevitable: on the contrary, antagonism between elitist religious-political movements and the community of ordinary believers is much more typical. The declaration by the founder of the Muslim Brotherhood in Egypt, Hassan al-Banna, (1965: 228) is relevant here: 'Our task is in fact nothing more than an offensive against widespread customs and a transformation of traditional practices.' The tendency to conflate these two phenomena stems from an unwillingness to comprehend the complex processes underlying all that is subsumed under the term 'Islamic fundamentalism'.

Political Islam has accompanied the process of secularisation and modernisation to which Islamic societies have been subject since the end of the nineteenth century. This phenomenon is not simply adherence to tradition, or a reaction to modernisation. It fuses local traditional elements with modernism in a quest for identity and meaning. The political-religious movements themselves have evolved and changed over time, beginning with a struggle to politicise Islam and adapt it to modern purposes. Among the contemporary political-religious movements in the Middle East, there are serious differences of opinion concerning the definitions and meanings of Islam, the modern state, and the methods of political action that will success-fully blend religion and state.

It is the modernist agenda that distinguishes political religion from religious conservatism, which does not suffer from the same sort of split personality. A conservative approach would either attempt to preserve the unity of religion and state (as in the case of the ultra-Orthodox communities in Judaism), or accept, willingly or unwillingly, the separation of the two. Either way, the conservative approach is essentially defensive, a strategy of regrouping and retreat to the stability of religious tradition.

Maxime Rodinson (1966) launched a campaign against traditional philological Orientalism, promoting a historicist line of Islamic scholarship. He attempted to prove that there is no distinctively Islamic direction of development, and no *homo islamicus*. By the same token, one cannot speak of a single unit called the 'Islamic world', any more than one can speak usefully of the 'Christian world'. This is also true for C. Gaerts in his *Islam Observed* (1968) and Albert Hourani in *The Islamic City* (1970). Edward Said (1978), went further to prove *homo islamicus* is a product and a tool of orientalism which is a discourse of power relations of domination and control.

We can say that 'Islam' (or Islams) in the modern era is a social phenomenon quite different from medieval 'Islam', even if political Islam claims otherwise. The cultural, political and social elements of a religion change even more dramatically than do its beliefs, which in any case are not themselves as stable as people seem to 'believe'. Political ideology can be understood only in a concrete social context. But whereas European history can provide contexts in which ideologies seem to derive essentially from local and internal social dynamics (Eurocentrism), ideologies in the East are inextricably bound up with influences from and reactions to foreign ideologies which negates any explanation based purely on local social dynamics, past and present. The centrism of the 'centre', although an ideology, is not fraudulent because it is backed by a dominant socio-economic structure. The centrism of the 'periphery' lacks this sort of backing. It is a reaction to a distorted mirror-image of the centrism of the 'centre'. Contrary to unquestioned and consumed myths of postindustrial societies, Western centrism is more 'authentic' than its Third World variants upon which 'authenticity' is usually imposed.

Modern Islams, though not all centrist, including political Islam, are not an exclusively local product but the outcome of ongoing conflicts and dialogues with the West, involving not only self and other but also images of self and other (Tibi 1988: 33–9).

An important difference between Islam and secular ideologies in Islamic countries lies in the fact that Islam has solid symbolic capital in folk religion, whereas other ideologies often must build from scratch. Still, popular Islam is no more than a potential foundation for political Islam, and does not serve it exclusively. Secular nationalist movements, to take one case, exploit Islamic myths in order to gain mass support: Nasser, Gaddafi, Saddam Hussein and even Assad all fought against political Islam in one form or another, while exploiting popular Islam. In the case of Nasserism the popular base of enlightened nationalism is still unparalleled in modern Arab History. The failure of Arab nationalism to build a solid political foundation in popular tradition must be related to the economic and social failures of the regimes and not to an alleged unintelligibility of their ideas for the 'Islamic masses'.

In any case, it is impossible to derive a description of a religious-political ideology directly from the religion concerned. One must examine instead the interplay of four factors: (a) the religion and religious tradition; (b) the socio-political situation; (c) the degree and type of secularisation; (d) interaction with other cultures – in the case of Islamic modernity, the encounter with Western colonial and post-colonial culture was an encounter with modernism.

Bassam Tibi explains the encounter-conflict between Western and Islamic culture in terms of anomie and acculturation, building on Maria Mies who broadened Durkheim's concept of anomie to cultural anomie. This she (Mies 1972: 26) describes as a phenomenon

> created when two cultural systems come into conflict ... when one system demonstrates dominance and is capable of preserving it ... and the members of the inferior system recognize this dominance and attempt to attain it, but are prevented from so doing by structural factors.

Political Islam, according to Tibi, is a counter-acculturation, a cultural retrospection. It is, in other words, a modern reaction to the failed synthesis of the two cultures. The repoliticisation of Islam, by this reckoning, offers 'salvation, in the form of an identity and a promise of future prosperity' (Tibi 1988: 44, 50). I would disagree on one point:

the repoliticisation of Islam occurred at the same time as its divorce from politics, at the moment when the tension between the socio-political and the private *within* religion was at its height. Tibi is in fact describing the conditions of the encounter between elitist political Islam and popular religion. The simple beliefs of popular religion resist assimilation within the modern culture (acculturation) or penetration by it. Yet even when these beliefs come into contact with political Islam or Arab nationalism, ordinary people do not turn into 'fundamentalists'. In his various studies M. Arkoun portrays a colourful picture of popular uncanonical religiosities which vary from place to place in Islamic countries and are influenced by local pre-Islamic traditions.[5] These religiosities are less variable in time than in place. They show more resistance to change than the elitist forms that seem more dogmatic and therefore more tenacious. In fact they are much more vulnerable to change and are the most poignant expression of this vulnerability.

A too-general definition of 'fundamentalism' conflates the conservative religious establishment, the *ulema* (authoritative experts on religious matters), with modern political Islam. For Munson (1988: 4), for example, the term fundamentalist 'has come to refer to anyone who insists that all aspects of life, including the social and the political, should conform to a set of sacred scriptures believed to be inerrant and immutable'. This criterion makes no distinction between religious conservatives of different sorts, and religious establishments of whatever faith become indistinguishable from religious-political movements.

Religious conservatism adopts a defensive attitude towards modernism. A religious establishment can cooperate with or oppose a regime that separates religion and state. It crosses the line to political religion the moment it goes on the offensive – that is, when it aspires to gain power or to change the regime in some way. Such movements are usually characterised by various degrees of hostility towards the religious establishment, and sometimes towards the theology it produces. They preach a return to the sacred writings themselves without the mediation of theologians. This hostility intensifies when the religious establishment functions as a legitimator of the regime, or the purveyor of religious rulings (*fatwas*) to justify rulers' actions. The Egyptian ulema establishments, for instance, does not accept change; nor are they capable of introducing or promoting changes which have not already permeated the ruling elites. When they do issue rulings in favour of change, they do so unwillingly (Crecelius 1972: 167–77).

Much depends on the relationship between the political and religious establishments. In the shadow of colonialism, the religious establishment was frequently forced to cooperate with political Islam as well as with the nationalist movement. In Nasser's time, for example, the religious establishment made common cause with the regime – willingly and unwillingly – against political Islam. With these reservations in mind, one can say that virtually every modern Islamic political movement has clashed with the religious establishment to some degree or other, just as it has conflicts with popular religion. The same holds true for Jewish political-religious movements in Israel, which are at odds with both popular religion and with conservative orthodoxy. According to the widespread definitions of fundamentalism, Gush Emunim and the ultra-Orthodox belong to the same camp. But Gush Emunim is a political-religious movement, whereas the ultra-Orthodox streams represent conservative religion. In both Islam and Judaism, there can be a meeting of popular religion, the religious establishment and political religion.

The religious establishment in Egypt, too, is experiencing far-reaching changes, reflected in the increasingly political positions adopted by the senior representatives of the University of al-Azhar, and especially in the new emphasis on social and political matters in Friday mosque sermons. In any case, defensiveness and a survival instinct have so far remained the most prominent features of such groups, more important than any desire to reunite religion and state.

A brief summary of my argument follows. First, following the secularisation model, two tendencies emerge: a type of religion that aspires to return to politics, and a brand of politics that seeks a return to sanctity. Second, these two phenomena are both modern and mutually contradictory. Third, political religion must not be confused with religion, nor can it be derived from it. Fourth, political religion should be distinguished from popular religion on the one hand, and from the religious establishment and religious conservatism on the other; this makes it possible to examine the conditions of their encounters with each other. Fifth, the modernism of Islamic political-religious movements is also manifested in a unique type of response to the encounter with modern cultures and realities.

## The Historicisation of Concepts

For many scholars, a review of the development of the political-religious doctrine of the modern Islamist movements begins with the writings of the Pakistani philosopher Abu al-A'la al-Mawdudi

(1913–79). Of particular importance are his first book, *Islamic Jihad*, and *Islamic Government*, the most important of the works he published in the 1939–41 period during which his religious-political thinking coalesced. As Israeli scholar Emmanuel Sivan describes it, al-Mawdudi's ideas came to Egypt via Sayyid Qutb, the spiritual father of the Islamic political movements in Egypt and architect of the revolution in the thinking of the Muslim Brotherhood. Qutb's book *ma'lim fi al-tariq* ('Stones along the way') became the gospel of the Jama'at al-Islamiya (Sivan 1986). Fahmi Jedaane draws our attention to the possibility that the Palestinian Islamist intellectual an-Nabhani in the early 1950s has had an underestimated influence on Qutb and later religious-political movements (Jedaane 1990: 267). An-Nabhani worked with tools and concepts similar to those of al-Mawdudi and Qutb.

Special attention to the historicisation of al-Mawdudi's and Qutb's basic concepts will convey a deeper understanding of the relationship between religion and state in Islamic thought, and between nationalism and Islam in the Arab context. Al-Mawdudi's starting point is the concept of the 'new *jahiliya*'. In Islamic history this concept – a dark age or a state of ignorance – refers to the situation that prevailed in the Arabian Peninsula prior to the advent of Islam. According to al-Mawdudi, however, the *jahiliya* is not a historically specific period but rather a cultural, social and psychological condition that obtains whenever people are estranged from the ways of God. Thus the *jahiliya* also refers to the contemporary period. When it does, it entails a greater danger than did primeval ignorance, since now it exists within Muslim society and is concealed behind formal Islam. The 'new *jahiliya*', more complex than the old, includes the superstitious beliefs and practices that have accumulated over centuries as well as an 'imported *jahiliya*' deriving from Western secular ideas.

The way out of this situation, for al-Mawdudi, is to return to *hakimiyat allah*, the rule of God, the source of political and social order in Muslim society. The Sharia, Islamic religious law derived from the Koran, and the Sunna, the words and deeds of the Prophet, are the basis for social order. These became keywords in the modern political-Islamic lexicon.

Al-Mawdudi's many books were translated into Arabic and his ideas reworked, especially with regard to whether the advance from *jahiliya* to *hakimiya* is evolutionary or revolutionary (along with differences of opinion in connection with each of these options). Does the Sharia permit rebellion against a Muslim ruler? What is the place of *jihad* in the transition to a society of believers? These and similar questions stand at the centre of the debate, turning Islam – at least for al-Mawdudi, Qutb, and their disciples – into a religion looking back to a time of utopia, yearning to re-establish a lost divine harmony and justice.

Some students of political Islam have been oblivious to the fact that al-Mawdudi's point of departure was the situation of the Muslim minority in colonial India during its two-pronged struggle for national secession and liberation from Britain. These circumstances were no less decisive in the fashioning of al-Mawdudi's thought than the concept of the 'new *jahiliya*'. Obviously the emergence and consolidation of a new nation distinct from the Indian nation could have been based on what was peculiar to Muslims – i.e. Islam – but this does not *ipso facto* make 'Islam' into a complete socio-political system.

Until al-Mawdudi's writings were adapted by Sayyid Qutb in Egypt, another type of political Islam reigned there, especially among the Muslim Brotherhood. The concept of the 'new *jahiliya*' was unknown, as was that of *hakimiyat allah*. Al-Mawdudi's ideas acquired weight in Egypt only in the heat of battle between the Muslim Brotherhood and Nasser's nationalist regime, which did not hesitate to use selected Islamic rulings against them.

When Hassan al-Banna founded the Muslim Brotherhood in Egypt in 1928, he spoke of Islam as both religion and state. He advocated an evolutionary path of education and gradual social change, though he did not refrain from violence when he saw fit. He did not designate Muslim society as being in a state of *jahiliya*. He spoke of religious law as a source of legislation and he called for restoration of the caliphate, which Kemal Atatürk had abolished in Turkey only five years before the founding of the Muslim Brotherhood. But he did not use the term *hakimiyah*. For al-Banna, the nation had to be Islamic, but this did not constitute a substitute for a local national identity. Al-Banna stressed the importance of Arab unity as a means to Islamic unity. A 'moderate' nationalism accompanied his 'moderate' political religion.

Modern political Islam endeavours to derive legitimacy for the idea of 'the rule of God' from the Koran. Emphasis on scripture is common to political-religious circles in Islam, Judaism and Christianity (Lazarus-Yafeh 1988: 35). The first use of this concept by an Islamic political group is attributed to the Kharijite sect (in the context of the seventh century, a political group was equivalent to a religious sect). The Kharijites renounced support for Caliph Ali ibn Abu Talib when he agreed to arbitration between his claims and those of Mu'awiyah ibn Abu Sufyan, governor of Damascus. In their opposition to arbitration (*tahkim*) they cited the motto '*la hukm illa hukm allah*' (there is no rule other than God's). In modern Arabic, *hukm* has taken on the meaning of regime or administration, and this has been retrospectively applied to Koranic passages. Its obtained philosophical meaning is clear, as are the implications of the idea of direct divine rule in the world: rejection of human freedom and consequently abrogation of responsibility for one's deeds. This age-old dispute extends throughout the history of religious thought. For our purposes, it is important to note only that in the Koran the word *hukm* originally bore no meaning or connotation of government. The liberal Egyptian judge and thinker Muhammad Said al-Asmawi (1987) asserts convincingly that in the Koran *hukm* means 'trial' or 'arbitration'. To this day, in spoken Arabic, *hakim* means judge.

Al-Asmawi also refers to the concept *amr*, which in modern Arabic means 'command' or 'order', as a term used to refer to government or political administration. Bernard Lewis (1988: 34) adds to the term *amr* the later root of *wly* with its derivatives *wali* and *wilaya*, which were used for 'rule' and 'administration'. A second word used in modern Arabic to refer to government or regime, *nizam* ('order', 'system'), does not appear in the Koran. When Islamic political movements speak today of *nizam hukm islami* (an Islamic system of government), they are expressing a formulation that never existed in the Koran or in the Sunna. The modern demand for social and political life to be governed according to *nizam islami* reflects an approach totally foreign to early Muslims (Smith 1978: 117).

Judge Asmawi and other liberal religious thinkers living in Muslim countries today are following the approach of Sheikh Ali Abd al-Raziq of al-Azhar, in particular his book *al-islam wa-usul al-hukm* ('Islam and the principles of government'), published in 1928 and so maligned in Islamist circles. This book, the first systematic formulation by a Muslim cleric in the modern era of a comprehensive secular view of the relationship between religion and state, makes five important points: first, there is no peculiarly Islamic method of government; second, there is no basis in religious law, or in the Koran or the Sunna, for the rule of the caliphate; third, in Islamic history the 'election' of caliphs usually took place by force or through heredity; fourth, Islam as a universal religion, cannot provide the basis for local government, nor can it be based on a local government; fifth, the administrative and governing functions of the Prophet Muhammad were not an integral part of his prophetic mission (Abd al-Raziq).

It is no mere coincidence that this secularist book by a leading cleric was published in the decade that saw the founding of the Muslim Brotherhood. Secularism and political religion are different outcomes of the same process.[7] At the same time, the Egyptian scholar and jurist al-Sanhuri coined the expression '*al-islam din wa-dawlah*' (Islam is the religion and the state). Even then the secularisation process had split the elitist religious sphere in two: one part wanted to return to politics via the repoliticisation of Islam, while the other remained steadfast to the obligation to live Islam as a religion that cannot order matters of society and state, that means actually being ordered by the state.

In the Muslim world, and especially in the Arab world and Pakistan, a fierce and complex debate about the application of the Sharia as the main source of legislation has pitted secularists, liberals (religious and otherwise) and leftists against the Islamist movements. On this point, the political-religious movements have managed to win the support of the religious establishment. Here too, however, there is a dispute within the Islamist movements: is the Sharia to be applied literally, or merely to serve as *a* source of legislation? And which of the four schools of commentary on the Sharia is to apply?

The category of Sharia itself has undergone far-reaching changes since the dawn of Islamic history. In the Koran, it means 'way' or 'path'. Subsequently it took on the sense of the principles of the Koran and the Sunna that regulate the affairs of Muslim society. Today Sharia is used in practice to signify all Islamic *fiqh*, that is the commentaries and branches of theology that have developed around the Koran and Sunna. Unlike the Koran and Sunna, however, *fiqh* is recognized as a human product, a cultural enterprise that arose as a function of changing historical circumstances.

Liberal Egyptian scholars, even those who support religious law as a source for legislation or as a special heritage that has a role to play in fashioning society, argue that the Muslim religion is not one of legislation and law – unlike Judaism, in which *halakhah* orders cultural relations down to the minutest detail. The Koran has 6,000 verses, of which 700 deal with religious laws governing *ubadah* and *mu'amalat* (i.e. matters between persons and God and matters between persons and their neighbours). Only 200 of these actually prescribe 'laws' dealing with matters of conjugal life, inheritance and criminal law. In addition, the validity of some verses is cancelled out by others, so that, all in all, there are no more than 80 verses that actually can be said to 'lay down the law' in any unequivocal sense. From these 80 verses Islamic law must derive the inspiration for its endeavour to order modern society and its problems.

Besides Shiite Iran, several Muslim countries have adopted the Sharia as the main source of legislation. What happened when they did?

In Sudan, Sharia was ostensibly adopted 'word for word' by the dictator Jaffar al-Numeiri, precisely at the time that his regime had brought the populace to the brink of starvation. In Pakistan, too, the Sharia was adopted as the main source of legislation, chiefly during the one-man rule of Zia ul-Haq. There, too, punishments were prescribed that in fact have no connection with the Koran or Sunna, but derive rather from later periods of the Muslim imperium. In Saudi Arabia, the Sharia was declared to be the country's sole constitution at the outset. In this sense Saudi Arabia became the first 'fundamentalist' country in the Arab world by declaring a fundamentalist doctrine, *Wahabism*, as its official doctrine. Nevertheless Islamist groups find it hard to detect the *hakimiyyat allah* in that country. Particularly perplexing is the luxurious life of the rulers and heads of the ruling clan, and their declared loyalty to Western interests.

Even in Egypt, which has a more modern and enlightened tradition of governance, Article 11 of the 1971 constitution states that the principles of the Sharia are 'a primary source of legislation'. At this period – which did not last very long – Sadat was trying to build a popular base for his regime against the Nasserists by appealing to the quasi-underground al-Jama'at al-Islamiyah. By the time a new constitution was adopted in 1980, it had already become difficult to stop the process. The article was modified to read that the principles of the Sharia are 'the chief source of legislation'. The Sharia is not the essence of Islam, but a historical product of the non-separation of religion and state under the Muslim imperium: the attempt to apply it as an ahistorical phenomenon in the present has led to the catastrophes in Sudan and Pakistan (Fudah 1988: 11–70).

The Sharia embodies no political or constitutional theory. Throughout the history of Islam, most *ulema* were divided into two main branches: one that issued *fatwa* (religious rulings) to justify the actions and decisions of the ruler, usually in retrospect, and another that distanced itself from matters of state and dealt with family law, conjugal rules and so on. The first harbingers of the transfer of religion to the realm of the individual can be traced to the time when religious law was relegated to the resolution of conjugal matters only. Even al-Mawardi's *al-ahkam al-sultaniya*, from the end of the Abbasid period, contains not political theory but rather a description of the situation prevailing under the Abbasids, a description that retrospectively justifies their activity and the way they were 'elected'. This type of theology (also to be found in al-Ghazali, the greatest of the Muslim theologians) is typified by a preference for the wicked ruler over the social anarchy that *fitnah* (rebellion) brings.

'Theories' of this sort arose alongside the conversion of the caliphate to a variety of royal dynastic regimes. Already at the beginning of the Umayyad period, an ideology of *al-mirja'ah* (postponement) emerged to justify unjust or sinful regimes. According to this concept, the Muslim believer remains part of the Muslim nation even if his deeds are sinful; he will pay for his sins in the next world. The same holds true for a sinful ruler; he owes no accounting to the community of believers.

Islamic theology thus mediated between God and secular power. In this it was no different from other theologies. In the lifetime of the Prophet Muhammad, and during part of the period of the first four caliphs, there was no need for such mediation since the ruler's explicit conduct constituted theology (in the sense that theology was an explanation of his conduct, at least such is the collective historical memory of the Muslim nation). They did not rule according to Sharia, but rather produced Sharia by ruling. When Islamic society split under the third caliph, Othman, the abstract identity between religion and state began to turn into a concrete identity. To borrow from Hegel: an identity is concrete insofar as it embodies distinction and potential contradiction. Religion in the service of the state does not simply mean religion is state, or Islam equals religion equals state, since there is already a fissure within the identity. Just as the germs of the privatisation of religion appear in its relegation to conjugal matters, so too the ideological potential of theology points to the possibility of separating religion and state. In light of this distinction, consider a concept frequently found among the political-religious movements, namely *nizam al-khalifah* (rule of the caliphate), which in itself constitutes an identity of contradictions between religion and politics and harbours within itself the seeds of the struggle between them.

The history of the caliphate as an institution is interesting for two reasons. First, the abolition of the institution under Kemal Atatürk in Turkey in 1924 spawned movements that called for its restoration, that is for a return to the harmony between religion and state. Second, in the eyes of political Islam, the abolition was the beginning of a new era of nation-states, replacing the 'Islamic nation' that had been united under Ottoman rule.

The first caliphate was meant to be in succession to the Prophet, not to God. The relevant Koranic verse applies the word caliph (heir) to Adam, whom God designated as his heir on earth. This verse provides an opening for humanistic explanations of 'Islam.' Neither in the Koran nor in the Sunna is there any formula designating the caliphate as the institution of government. Of the first four caliphs (the Golden Age, according to political Islam), only one died a natural death, and the reigns of the last two were characterized by social and political unrest. The third caliph, Othman, whose reign saw the first revolt in the provinces (especially in Egypt), was the first to issue a pronouncement linking the institution of the caliphate with divine right. When a delegation of his opponents from Egypt demanded his abdication, he replied (at least so tradition has it): 'I will not cast off the garment in which God has clothed me' (al-Reis 1966:42). Despite this, the period of the first four caliphs, including Othman, has remained in the collective Islamic memory as a period of harmony, of identity between religion and state, as a period in which divine justice prevailed. These caliphs did not use Islam as a political theory; they created it. Islam as a divine justification of government begins with the rupture of the Muslim nation and the struggle for power. When the Muslim imperium subsequently turned into a state ruled by a king (caliph) who bequeathed his function to his descendants, Muawia, the first Umayyad caliph, asserted: 'the earth is God's property ... and I am God's caliph. What I take is mine and what I leave for the people is only by my right'. Thus in Islam, too, rule by divine right began with the inauguration of monarchy. When 'harmony' prevailed, there was no need for a divine regime (*hakimiyat allah*). Latent within this use of religion as an instrument in the hands of the state, in the shadow of the unity of religion and state, are the seeds of secularisation.

Starting in the tenth century CE, and for a relatively long period thereafter, the Muslim world was ruled simultaneously by three dynasties, each asserting its right to the caliphate: the Abbasids in Baghdad, the Fatimids in Tunis and then Egypt, and the Umayyads in Andalusia. From 935 on, the authority of the caliphs was limited to ratifying the mandate of the true rulers in the provinces, the sultan assuming the status of true king and the caliph being king in name only. This situation continued until the Mongols overran Baghdad in 1258, after which the caliph became a sort of abstract ruler, a source of legitimacy, who sanctioned the 'real' rule of the sultan.

The foregoing is not meant to ignore the unique nature of the caliphate, which combined religion and state. Rather, I wish to emphasise the general dimensions of the identity of religion and state in Islam. An emphasis on the unique features of the caliphate, both when it exercised effective power and when it had lost it, turns it into a myth. It is, in fact, the concrete Islamic embodiment of the concrete institutional identity of religion and state. Its uniqueness should not make us unable to abstract and form general ideas which are a precondition for comparative thinking. Simple generalisation from the particular or particularisation of the universal only creates only myths.

Ever since the elimination of this symbol of the identity of religion and state in 1924, political Islam has never ceased to demand its restoration, and with it 'the unity of the Islamic nation'. Different, even contradictory things were meant by the proponents of this unity: reform, revolution, and Islamicisation of existing regimes in their quest for legitimacy. Obviously Jaffar al-Numeiri in Sudan, Zia ul-Haq in Pakistan, and the Saudi rulers in Saudi Arabia (the only survivor among them) have failed to recapture the lost 'harmony' between religion and state. Of particular interest is the conclusion of one Muslim scholar concerning the relationship between religion and state in Saudi Arabia:

> Saudi Arabia is turning into a state with a civilian government despite its fundamentalist leanings. The state has extended its jurisdiction to other areas that were formerly bound up with religion and the religious establishment. Even the *ulema* have become appendages to the civil service; the laws of the country regulate their activity. Out of the exclusivity of government and the exclusivity of its connection with the national treasure and its struggle to retain its independence, it does not allow an independent religious authority to exist or to compete with it for the loyalty of the citizens. Hence the state has extended its authority over the religious sector and has made use of the *ulema* in order to acquire legitimisation for its policies. (al-Yassini 1987: 14–15)

Saudi Arabia has been and remains the main source of funding for non-radical political-Islamic movements (such as the Muslim Brotherhood), especially when they fight nationalism or 'Arab socialism'.

In this context, I find most strange the claims of Bernard Lewis (174: 159–60) to the effect that Islam cannot accept the separation of religion and state, and that for Muslim conservatives God alone is the ruler. The urge to unity is itself the product of separation, and an awareness of its absence. Ahmad ibn Hanbal, the leading representative of the most stringent of the four schools of interpretation of Islamic religious law, quoted the following saying of the Prophet: 'Anything relating to your religion you shall bring to me, but in your temporal affairs you are more expert.' The revival of the notion of inseparability of government and religious law in Islam began with the repoliticisation of religious symbols by modern political-religious movements, as part of their search for identity in a world changing at a giddy pace. The encounter with modernity spawned concepts and connotations that were projected on to the past. In this way, political Islam looks back to a utopia.

## The Islamic Nation and Arab Nationalism

The original meaning of *al-ummah al-islamiyah* is 'community of believers'. Only in modern times, when *ummah* was used to render the word 'nation' in the European sense of a political unit and to represent a new political reality and consciousness, did it take on the connotations of the latter. This sense was then anachronistically projected on to each appearance of the term in classical Islamic literature, and received unexpected support when the first modern state founded on a religious basis, Pakistan, was created in 1947. A year later, in 1948, when the state of Israel was founded, political Islam was not especially impressed by Zionism's self-image as a secular national movement; it saw Zionism as buttressing its claims that it is possible to establish a state on the basis of a religious 'nation'. Modern *ummah* was projected retrospectively on to Islamic history to make the community of believers mean a modern political nation. This is total opposed to the process described by Bernard Lewis (1988: 42) in which Arab borrowing of a religious category seems to be the main development. If we go back to Lewis's early studies (1968: 70) we find his view that the main identification for Arabs remains 'Islam'. Borrowing a holy category to represent a modern state of affairs was actually meant to indicate the absence or at least insignificance of Arab nationalism.

Modern Arab nationalism emerged in the nineteenth century and claimed an organised form in national associations and conferences and in the revolt which broke out in 1916. As a result of the balance of power in the post-First World War era, Arab nationalism was unable to find expression in a nation-state, that is in the European sense of political unit. Do the Arabs constitute a nation? Does their aspiration for political unity in a state make them into a nation? The scholastic debate around this question resembles nothing so much as the debate that raged a century ago as to whether there was a German nation. What is not in doubt is that an Arab nationalism has developed, based on a common language, territorial continuity, a collective historical memory and a shared belief in the existence of an Arab nation.

For a non-historical approach the confrontation between Arabism and 'Islam', in both its overt and covert forms, dates back to the first Arab Muslim conquests outside the Arabian Peninsula and the conversion to Islam of non-Arab peoples who became part of the imperium. In Islamic Arab culture, a true Hegelian contradiction existed between the universalist pretensions of Islam and its Arab distinctiveness, on the one hand, and Islam's contribution to the coalescence of the Arab identity on the other. The dynamic underlying this contradiction gave rise to an extremely creative cultural synthesis alongside harsh struggles and conflicts, in which the various non-Arab Muslim peoples fought in the name of equality for all Muslims against Arab dominion in the imperium.

The Iraq–Iran war of the 1980s brought back an awareness of the conflict between 'Arabism' and *shu'ubiyah* (a reference to the discontent of non-Arab Muslims in the Islamic empire with Arab domination) via the use made by Baghdad and Tehran of myths drawn from collective memory for the sake of political propaganda. Obviously, the struggle for control of the Gulf region is nothing like the struggle between Arabism and *shu'ubiyah* in the context of the Islamic empire. As a general rule, Arab nationalist leaders use Islamic myths because the Islamic imperium is perceived as the Golden Age of the Arab nation.[8] The conflict with Israel, in particular after the 1967 conquest of East Jerusalem, gave tremendous momentum to the deployment of Islamic myths. But even without taking the Palestine question into account, it is easy to discern that secular Arab leaders find it difficult to declare themselves secular, as Atatürk permitted himself to do in his campaign to disestablish the caliphate as part of the consolidation of modern Turkey.

What, then, is the relationship between Arabism and Islam in the modern age? Did Arab nationalism arise at the same time throughout the Arab world, a result of the consolidation of an urban middle class spawned by contacts with the West and modernism, or did it have more specific origins in Syria, Lebanon and Palestine? The first confrontations between Arabs and the Ottoman empire – that were viewed as such – erupted in Greater Syria, following the Turkish nationalist revolt of 1908, and were directed against the concomitant attempt to give the empire a distinctively Turkish coloration. In their modern form, Turkish and Arab nationalism are twins: they were born during the same period, when a modern urban middle class grew up among both peoples and developed local interests and a yearning for Western education, and came under the ideological influence of European nationalism. Both movements dismantled Islamic unity and disavowed the *ummah*. The Arab struggle began with the demand for local autonomy, but quickly moved to calls for secession from the empire and the establishment of an Arab state.

Muslim historians who support political Islam lay full 'responsibility' for the birth of Arab nationalism on the shoulders of Arab Christian thinkers in Syria. Indeed, the Arab Christian intelligentsia in Syria did seek a common bond with the Muslim majority to promote separatism from the Ottomans. The Arab Christian intelligentsia also had greater exposure to Western influence, including nationalist ideologies. Yet there were also many Muslims among the founders of Arab nationalism, including clergymen such as the Syrian Abd al-Rahman al-Kawakibi, and later secularists such as Sat'a al-Husri. Both the Arab Muslim and Arab Christian intelligentsia went through the same process, but in the case of the Christians its manifestations were more acute, owing to their circumstances. The urban middle classes, which carried the national idea in its 'moderate' versions, mostly comprised Sunni Muslims.

One can discern two clear streams in Arab ideology. The first developed a nationalist ideology independent of Islam, one which relates to Islam as, at most, a cultural heritage. The second views religion as a key element. The earliest proponents of Arab nationalism were largely influenced by Western liberal tradition (which they translated into Arabic) and worked out their own liberal nationalist political outlook. Only after the beginnings of the anti-colonial confrontation with the 'democratic West' did Arab nationalist thinking develop in the direction of the sort of romantic nationalism adopted by al-Husri (Tibi 1988: 40) and Aflaq. By the time conflict had broken out with the colonial powers – France in North Africa, Syria and Lebanon; Britain in Egypt, Palestine and Iraq – Arab nationalism had already developed as an ideology with multiple streams. It was at that point that Arab nationalism began to come into contact with popular religion, as well as with the religious establishment. In North Africa, where there were no large Christian minorities, no struggle against the modern Turkicisation of the Ottoman empire, Islam came to play a major role in the formation of nationalism. At the time of national formation, North African countries were colonised by foreign un-Islamic powers.[9]

In Egypt, on the other hand, we find a more classic picture. The country enjoyed formal independence, the nationalist movement retained its liberal-democratic character through the period of anti-British struggle, and two currents of political Islam developed alongside it. The first called for reform and modernisation of Islam and cooperated with the nationalist movement, whereas the second developed a political Islam outside the nationalist movement and began to advocate the restoration of Islamic unity and its symbol, the caliphate. This first organised version of political Islam saw national independence as just a step on the path to an Islamic state.

Secular nationalist ideology spread through Arab countries after their liberation from colonial rule, especially in the 1950s and 1960s, with the rise to power of regimes that espoused this ideology and embroidered emblems of Arab unity on their flags. The new Arab nationalist states viewed organised religious forces as a hindrance which opposed the new state institutions that arose under the control of the officer caste and were consolidated under the aegis of new middle-class elites.

> By distancing Islam from the political field the state sought to preserve it in a congregational, educational and private sphere, and to block its broader public ideological relationship to the state itself as well as to social experience on the national level. (Gilsenan 1985: 177)

Arab nationalism was neutral on matters of religion during short periods in its history. It separated religion from state, but without adopting for itself the classic European model.

There is no doubt that the concept of the 'Arab nation' (and even Arab nationalism) has undergone a process of secularisation for three reasons:

(a)  the historical origins of the concept in the struggle against the Muslim Ottoman empire;
(b)  the social agents that transformed the abstract concept into reality in concrete social struggles: the bourgeoisie, and the intelligentsia with aspirations for national independence that sprang from it;
(c)  the political subject itself: Arabs, both Muslims and Christians, were separated from other Muslims by nationalist ideology; Islam became an element in their national identity, rather than the other way around.

Secularisation of the term *ummah* also gave rise to the tendency of political religion to repoliticise the concept 'Islamic nation', and to perceive it as a political-religious entity, as opposed to the political-national Arab nation. The sanctification of values in the secular sphere clashed with the repoliticisation of values in the religious sphere.

Opposition to Arab nationalism when it was at its zenith, when it was associated with concepts such as Arab socialism, nationalisation, anti-imperialism and leadership of the non-aligned bloc, stemmed chiefly from conservative forces supported by Western powers. For a relatively long period, the feudal-tribal (in terms of their political structure) regimes appeared to be the defenders of Islam against secular Arab ideology. The same conservative regimes that once defended *iklimiyah* (localism or local patriotism) against Arab unity now championed the universalist ideology of political Islam. At the height of this dispute, in 1966, Saudi Arabia organised the Islamic Conference Organisation, intended to include all countries with a Muslim majority. At first Nasser refused to participate, only to change his mind after the rout of 1967. This order of affairs is symptomatic of the relationship between 'Islam' and Arab nationalism in the 1960s and 1970s: one waxes when the other waned. Israel's victory in 1967 translated into a defeat for pan-Arabism. This was reflected in the Egyptocentric attitudes of Sadat and his advisers, in the rise of Saudi Arabia as a major force in the Arab world, and in the growing power of political Islam as an alternative ideology.

The seeds of the ideological crisis of Arab nationalism and the socio-economic crisis of the Arab regimes antedated the 1967 defeat, and may even have been one of its causes. But this crisis did not affect the sense of national affiliation among the mass of people, which continued to coexist intermingled with popular religion (a contradiction between nationalism and religion is alien to folk religiosity). Among the Arab nationalist intelligentsia there occurred a process of polarisation and the development of new currents relating to questions touching on the political structure of the state, democratic government, economic independence and so forth. In this context, a critical relationship has been evolving since the 1970s towards the region's Islamic heritage as well as to the break with it.

Emmanuel Sivan (1990) provides a detailed description of the attitude of Islamic political movements to Arab nationalism, especially in the 1960s and 1970s. He quotes Sa'id Hawa (1979: 92–3), a prominent leader of the Muslim Brotherhood in Syria, who defines Arabism as a secular religion:

Affiliation to a nationality as such is quite a natural phenomenon. But what is objectionable is that when someone is asked, 'What is your creed?' one answers: 'Arab.' For that Arab that he is Muslim, or Christian, or Jewish. Ethnic identity must have no impact on one's beliefs, perceptions, and mores. This grave error ends up making nationalism a substitute for Islam.

This stance is quite typical of the thinking of modern Islamic political movements, but is not typical of the community of believers as a whole in any period.

Radical Islamic movements, especially those active in Egypt and Syria, distribute vast numbers of pamphlets, books and posters protesting against what they term 'state idolatry' – things such as saluting the flag, patriotic songs, visits to the Tomb of the Unknown Soldier. In the Middle Eastern context, any observer will clearly see the contrast between these elements in the Arab world and the political-religious movements in Israel whose publications disclose a hybrid attitude of hatred mixed with respect for the state of Israel, viewed as a Jewish religious state, possessing a secular character but a religious definition.

Most historians date the beginning of the modern era in Islamic history to Napoleon's invasion of Egypt, even though this event really marks the beginning of modern history in Egypt only. But given the influence of Egypt in the Arab world, and against the backdrop of the major changes that shook the Ottoman empire at the beginning of the nineteenth century, we can accept this starting point. The Islamic revival during the deep and prolonged internal crisis that beset the Ottoman empire coincided with the confrontation with modernisation and with the importation of ideas from the West. Rather than divide the process into stages and periods, I will emphasise programmatic differences.

The first stage saw the emergence of the ideological current which we may call 'fundamentalism' in the original meaning of the term, in that it aspired to a return to the pure tenets of Islam, and was subject to minimal external influence but with internal mechanisms predominant. Among its features were the fight against superstition and legend, the rejection of any mediation between persons and God through saints or cults of saints, and stringent explanations of the Koran and Sunna. This current included the Wahhabis in the Arabian Peninsula and later the Sanussis in Libya and the Mahdists in Sudan. At the more cosmopolitan cultural centre, another current called for reorganisation of the empire (the Sultans Selim III and Mahmud II in Istanbul and Muhammad Ali in Egypt). The first current erupted on the margins of the Ottoman empire. The second was characterised by an attempt to introduce institutional reforms and to modernise the administration of the empire, or parts of it, in the context of a unity of religion and state. These were perhaps the last attempts at Islamic revival in this context.

The second stage of the revival began with important thinkers such as Jamal al-Din al-Afghani (1839–96) and his Egyptian disciples,

Muhammad Abduh (1849–1905) and Muhammad Rashid Rida (1865–1935). These thinkers founded an impressive enterprise devoted to the renewal of Islam and its adaptation to modernism, and opened the door to more liberal interpretations (*ijtihad*) of the Koran and Sunna. Al-Afghani called for unity under the umbrella of a modern enlightened Islam (al-Bishri 1989: 152–63). He understood that modernisation had to take into account Arab national identity, the dominant cultural factor in the Ottoman empire. He called on the Ottoman caliph to make Arabic the official language of the empire (al-Afghani 1986: 161–2). Around the same time, one of the fathers of Arab nationalism, Sheikh Abd al-Kawakibi, called for the replacement of the Turkish caliph by an Arab one.

A reformed Islam evolved in Egypt that saw Arabism as one of its components; it coexisted with Egyptian secular nationalism which generally accepted both Islam and Arabism among its main components, while in Syria an Arab nationalism arose that viewed Islam as one of its components alongside Syrian nationalism representing itself as Arab nationalism. The path that leads from al-Afghani to Rashid Rida tends towards the growing politicisation of 'Islam' as a conservative power, a detailed concern with social organisation, and involvement with the internal contradictions of Egyptian society, which had begun to experience the schizophrenia engendered by the emergence of modern institutions and modern education alongside a conservative tradition and religious education.

The national movement that opposed the British occupation, the Wafd party, adopted a liberal secular approach, while the Muhammad Abduh – Rashid Rida tendency supported a more severe political Islam. Rashid Rida began to rely intensively on the religious rulings and commentaries of the school of Ibn Taymiyya, the fourteenth-century Islamic philosopher who was the first to permit struggle (jihad) against a Muslim ruler and who made jihad against infidels into a religious precept. In our own day, the entire legacy of Ibn Taymiyya was resurrected by Sayyid Qutb in the 1960s and the Islamic groups (the Jama'at) in the 1970s and 1980s. Al-Afghani began by jumping headlong into modernity, and Rida ended with seclusion and strict interpretations. As the secularisation of society intensified, the Islamic revival developed either compromising or rejectionist attitudes to modernity but lost its potential to lead the process.

The third current arises at the end of the era of al-Afghani, Abduh and Rida, with the founding of the Muslim Brotherhood in Egypt. This heralded the beginning of the history of political Islam as an organised movement. The organisation attained its greatest popularity in the 1940s. Supporters of the Muslim Brotherhood came mainly from the lower middle class, especially from Egypt's small towns, and also from villagers who had migrated to the cities, but at its peak it managed to penetrate all levels of the Egyptian people. It organised an underground (*al-jihaz al-sirri*) that worked alongside it but did not preach violence as a means to bring about the Islamicisation of society and state. The history of the Muslim Brotherhood abounds with tension between the political leadership and the more militant underground leadership, and there were serious outbreaks of violence in their struggle against the Wafd regime of the 1940s. The organisation forged an alliance with the monarchy against the liberal-secular Wafd but, as the Brotherhood's strength grew, it found itself confronting the king as well. Its leader fell victim to this confrontation in 1949, after the organisation was outlawed.

In the writings of the founder and leader of the Brotherhood, Hassan al-Banna (n.d.: 113–14), we find the slogan that Islam is 'cult and leadership, religion and state, spirituality and practical application, prayer and jihad, rule and obedience, Koran and sword'. Al-Banna was willing to cooperate with Arab nationalism, or to accept the idea of Arab unity from an overall Islamic perspective and from the position of an independent organisation – that is, not as a part of the national movement.

In his letter to the Fifth Conference of the Muslim Brotherhood, al-Banna (1965: 74–8) wrote:

National liberation is a stage in the process of human development towards universalism. Any national revival, national entity and regional unity are a step on the road to the yearned-for universality. Universality, or humanity, is our lofty aim and the final goal of the series of reforms. The world will attain it by necessity. Every merger of nations and mingling of races and peoples, every alliance of the weak ... all these pave the way for the universalist idea that replaces national *shu'ubiyah*, in which men believed in the past.

The attempts to arrange a compromise between Arab nationalism and Islam through the separation of religion and nationalism did not last long. When a faction of the Muslim Brotherhood published al-Banna's letter in 1977, the following comment was appended:

At the time that the national and patriotic movements were awakening, it appeared to some Muslim preachers that it was possible to reach an understanding with these movements. Practical experience has shown that these two doctrines can never meet, because political Islam is a universalist divine religion, intended for all mankind, whereas those dogmas are racist dogmas, created by men in this world.

The compromise between the political-religious and the national movements lasts until the rise of regimes that openly espouse a nationalist ideology. The conversion of nationalist ideology into ruling ideology shunts religions to the sidelines of the political arena. Political religion aspires to a state, and the struggle becomes a struggle for power.

In 1954, all parties except the Muslim Brotherhood were outlawed in Egypt. That same year saw the eruption of a serious dispute between the Brotherhood and the Revolutionary Council, which took on a violent character after an attempt on Nasser's life the same year. A fierce dispute arose within the Brotherhood concerning its relations with the secular national government, a dispute that led to a number of schisms within the ranks of the organisation. Nasser's regime persecuted the Muslim Brotherhood with a ruthless thoroughness, especially at the zenith of his popularity during and after the 1956 Suez war. For some time it appeared that political Islam had been eradicated. This was the epoch of Arab nationalism.

The remnants of the Muslim Brotherhood fled to neighbouring countries and entered into an overt alliance with conservative forces like the Saudi regime. The Muslim Brotherhood took a long time to recover from the onslaught of Nasser's Arab unity, as well as from their image as Saudi allies and foes of Arab nationalism. (In the 1930s and 1940s, long before the confrontation with Nasser, large Muslim Brotherhood organisations sprang up throughout the Arab world, especially in Sudan, Syria and Jordan. They were influenced by the Egyptian organisation. They never managed to rival it in terms of popular support and organisational ability, however, and the crisis of the Egyptian organisation afflicted them as well.)

After the 1967 defeat, which the Brotherhood perceived as divine retribution for the sins of Arab nationalism, the domestic social crisis threatening the Arab populist regimes grew worse. In Egypt, Sadat released those jailed for membership of the Brotherhood and allowed the organisation to publish a journal and to operate in the open. In Syria, the Brotherhood established links with the bourgeoisie, especially the merchants of Damascus, Hama and Aleppo, and with the landowners who had suffered through agrarian reform. 'Arab socialism', with all its bureaucratic apparatus, was in serious crisis. It had managed, at a heavy cost, to build an economic infrastructure which had become paralysed and stagnant. Conservative forces mounted intensive efforts to change the regimes.

The regimes that came to power after the 1967 defeat only made matters worse. Their swift about-face from distorted state capitalism to a mixed economy engendered a process of impoverishment that shook the roots of society, sparking migration from the villages to the cities, causing unemployment, and creating a new class of brokers between world markets and local consumers – a function formerly filled by the state. These newly rich comprised social elements who had thrived on the destruction of the public sector and the privatisation of foreign trade and major construction contractors, and who were even more alienated from the people than was the military bureaucracy, which at least had been able to assert an ideology and claim limited economic reforms.

At a popular level, on the other hand, there was a massive Islamic revival, manifest in dress, attendance at mosques, and so forth. The regimes had tossed out one ideology and had failed to supply an alternative. Now they thought to compensate for this by increasing the slots for religious programming on government broadcasting channels, by intensifying their use of religious jargon, by investing money in the religious establishment, and by building mosques. This was like pouring oil on a burning fire, and a conflagration was not long in coming. In the late 1970s, the Muslim Brotherhood staged a coup attempt in Syria, Numeiri adopted the Sharia in Sudan, and Zia ul-Haq came to power in Pakistan with the support of the Jama'at al-Islamiyah there. The Islamic movements also spread in Lebanon and North Africa. The Iranian revolution in 1979 was the high water mark of the growing power of political Islam, although it had a different starting point and direction, it provided new options to the political-religious awakening throughout the Islamic world.

The way to understand political Islam as a modern phenomenon must be through an understanding of the modern milieu in existing Muslim societies – their economies, politics and cultures in the broad senses of the term. The modern political-religious movements are the outcome of the distorted process of secularisation to which Islamic societies were exposed, of the economic crisis that capped their encounters with international capitalism, and of the crisis of identity engendered by the cultural encounter with modernism.

## Islamic Political Religion in Crisis

In the early 1980s, the internal configuration of the Islamist movement became extremely complicated. Groups and subgroups, parties and factions spread through all the countries of the Middle East. Sometimes the same name was used by several organisations of different types – Islamic Jihad, for instance. Even in the eyes of the adherents of political Islam, the proliferation and diversification of the Islamist movements are marks of failure as well as of success. The diversification stems not only from different conditions and different personalities, or from dissimilarities of cultural and class origins, but also from the fact that disparate and sometimes contradictory social, economic, and political ambitions began to assume Islamist formulations or to be justified in Islamist terms. One cannot deny that this represents a certain accomplishment for political Islam. Recently, however, some members of the Islamist intelligentsia have begun to criticise the inability of political Islam to present a clear solution to the problems that preoccupy developing societies.[10] Diversity also indicates an absence of unity. Those who claim to possess absolute truth themselves demonstrate that there is no such thing. This is most obvious in their varying and sometimes even contradictory interpretations of the Sharia.

Is political Islam in crisis today? Yes, with regard to how it has operated thus far. We must not conclude, though, that political Islam is spent. We can observe spectacular successes in the Maghreb, notably in Algeria and Tunisia, which introduce a fourth phase that remains beyond our discussion in this chapter. It has managed to link up with popular religion in Jordan, in the West Bank and Gaza, and among Palestinian citizens of Israel. In all these cases, however, we see an interesting synthesis or compromise with Arab nationalism and with modernisation. Political Islam's record in governing Sudan, Pakistan and Iran does not appear to have been particularly brilliant, not only as regards matters such as freedom of expression and democracy, but chiefly with regard to social issues.

The radicalisation in the attitude of the Islamist organisations in the late 1970s and early 1980s turned them once again into elitist movements, intensified their internal rifts, and distanced the most radical groups from the community of believers, i.e. from popular religion. This is why the radical groups are again making use of methods that bring them closer to the masses, such as incitement against religious minorities (Copts in Egypt, for example), the Western lifestyle of the upper classes and the pro-Western policies of the political regimes. In the final analysis, however, the fruits of the intensification of ethnic tension are garnered chiefly by the conservatives or moderate Islamists like the Muslim Brothers, who are able to propose a social compromise.

The plethora of Islamist groups that evolved in Egypt in the early 1970s had two main sources. One was the schisms within the ranks of the Muslim Brotherhood after its confrontation with Nasser, which had already begun inside Egyptian jails. The Takfir wa-al-hijrah was formed by prison inmates: it broke off all contact with the Brotherhood within the prison, even staying away from them during prayers (*hijrah* means 'migration', alluding to the Prophet Muhammad's escape to Medina when the persecution of Muslims in Mecca grew unbearable), and sought to sever all ties with modern phenomena.

The second source was the Jama'at al-Islamiyah (Islamist groups) that organized in Egyptian universities with the government's blessing at that time. In this context one should bear in mind the introduction of free secondary and higher education by the Arab regimes, an innovation that brought the universities within reach of the lower classes.

Some of these groups established their own peculiar culture, which included total obedience to the leader, and prepared themselves for jihad against infidel society. The radicalism of the methods adopted by this organisation in its 'return to pure Islam' is not particularly typical. But the concept of an infidel society (*jahaliya*) and the licence to wage jihad against a Muslim ruler spread among the student adherents of the Muslim Brotherhood as well, especially at the peak of their traumatic tortures inside Nasser's prisons. Jihad against Israel did not particularly impress these young men: they saw their main task as the liberation of Muslim society from the rule of the impious. This task had to be completed before they could turn their attention to the enemy outside.

The many studies of the social origins of the activists in these organizations reveal a profile that is also typical of Islamist activists outside Egypt: they come from the lower middle class; they have a university education, usually in the natural sciences, engineering or medicine; and although they are city-dwellers when they join the organisation, their origins are usually rural (Ayabi 1980: 443; Ibrahim 1980: 488).

This profile is hardly surprising. First, the lower middle class is most vulnerable to the processes accompanying the introduction of capitalism and most susceptible to the alienating influences of secularisation. Their impoverishment engenders a bitterness and loss of faith in the social order. Second, higher education intensifies this bitterness by holding out the promise of a better social standing, rising above the structural impediments to fulfilment of ambitions and to satisfaction of minimal daily needs. A university education in the natural sciences develops familiarity with the scientific-technological face of modernism without a concomitant exposure to its spiritual content, and without any provision of the tools for working through the encounter with it. What they take for the spirit of modernisation is represented by the depraved manifestations of moral licence by the newly rich. Third, the transition from village to town adds a further element of anonymity, alienation and loss of identity. They live in the city and yet not in the city, as in a village which has lost its rural intimacy without achieving the individualism of the city.

Young adults who have left the villages usually live in slums on the outskirts of the metropolis. There, in the mosques of the suburban slums whose very architecture proclaims a terrible loss of identity, the migrants find a welcome and begin organising themselves. Structural barriers keep these embittered students from integrating into the affluent classes that are reaping the fruits of modernisation. But modernity itself, higher education, the demand for political organisation – these are what provide them with the means to do battle against the status quo. They take up an offensive posture, looking back to a past utopia. This escape is not conducted as a retreat but as an attack. Those who espouse it are not conservatives but rather a unique product of modernity: modern individuals with a split and alienated consciousness, enlightened persons alienated from 'enlightenment'.

The German sociologist Niklas Luhmann (1982: 115) assigns two functions to religion: (a) defining the undefined, especially in crises of identity; and (b) cushioning disappointments. Religion has classically played these two roles in the suburbs of large cities throughout the Arab world. Luhmann's analysis can be refined: as long as religion cushions disappointments, we remain in the domain of folk religion; political religion goes over to the offensive.

Latent in the self-understanding of members of the Islamic groups is an enormous and special hatred for the United States and everything it represents. One could see this during the Gulf crisis, when confrontation with the Americans and opposition to their involvement overshadowed all enmity towards the Iraqis and opposition to Saddam Hussein. The West and its 'agents' are held responsible for the social situation, especially after the adoption of an open-market economy, and also for the repeated 'dishonouring' of the Islamic nation through unqualified support for Israel. The trauma of 1967 plays an important role, but the Camp David 'capitulations' and the Israeli presence in East Jerusalem have also become symbols of the humiliation to which 'the Islamic nation' has been subjected. Both the opposition to the United States and the hostility towards Israel reinject a dimension of Arab nationalism into the position of political Islam. Despite these organisations' disavowal of nationalism and national interest, we find that the actions that stirred identification in the Arab world were those that took up national issues, such as the assassination of Sadat and Hizbollah's campaign against Israel and the US in Lebanon after 1982. For the general population in Islamic society, popular religion coexists with feelings of national affiliation. The modern manifestations of anti-nationalist elitist political religion occupy the fringes of the religious sphere and the margins of the political map.

Out of the crisis of both secular Arab nationalism and anti-nationalist political Islam we can already detect a synthesis emerging with strong tendencies to continue the interrupted reforms of the nineteenth century. This synthesis is driving Islamist movements to defend national interests, to represent national issues and to reform the relationship with state institutions. Ex-leftists and nationalists who joined the Islamic tendencies during the last decade have translated to ideas of liberation and unity into the language of Islam. Leading figures in the Islamic movements, like Hasan al-Turabi and Rachid al-Ghanouchi, are engaged in an attempt to introduce reform as a social, cultural and political project.

Meanwhile major Arab regimes are engaged in a fierce struggle of life or death with radical militant groups. But they cannot launch the struggle in the name of nationalism, secularism and justice, but of naked will to power. The uncompromising Islamic groups represent little but deep frustration and rejection of alienating realities. On the other side, national and Islamic forces which have any message or project are looking for a common language. These are not the Islamic and national currents we once knew; there has been a development. The 'end of history' either did not pass through this region or went unnoticed.

## Notes

1 The process of separation was accomplished more easily in the Jewish-Christian-Islamic tradition, whose theism had already established a divide between God and the world. But one must not confuse secularisation with the removal of God from the world. The very possibility of defining religion is peculiar to this tradition. A Hindu, for instance, would find it an impossible task.

2 Exceptions are those countries where historically there has been an overlap between local patriotic nationalism and the contribution of religion to national identity, especially when a country is surrounded by others professing other faiths. Hence the special

affiliation between Poles and Catholicism. Even here, however, the overlap is more between religious conservatism and Polish patriotism. Catholic fundamentalism contains a universal element that stands against any absolute valorisation of local patriotism.

3   Journalist Dilip Hiro asserts that

> it is in the nature of any major religion to revitalise itself periodically. But Islam is special, because it is more than a religion. It constitutes a complete social system that embraces all those who have accepted Islam. It is indeed civilisation that applies to all times and places. (Hiro 1989: 1)

The same author's definition of fundamentalism is general and ahistorical, as are many of his statements: 'Fundamentalism is the term used for the effort to define the fundamentals of a religious system and adhere to them.'

4   Compare with M. al-Jabiri (1987: 40).
5   Compare with M. Arkoun (1990: 115).
6   'Islamic groups' is an Egyptian term for the movements that arose alongside the Muslim Brotherhood and split from it in the early 1970s.
7   The secularisation manifested in Abd al-Raziq's book was a reaction to an attempt of al-Azhar and the 'palace' to restore the caliphate by declaring King Fuad of Egypt a caliph. This kind of secularisation is directed against the state's exploitation of religion and thus motivated by deep religious feelings.
8   Sivan (1988) surveys such myths.
9   In his debate with Hasan Hanafi, al-Jabiri emphasises several times that in the Maghreb as opposed to the Mashreq even for elites Islam and Arabism meant almost the same thing for a long period of time (al-Jabiri and Hanafi 1990).
10  See al-Nafisi (1989). This volume, edited by al-Nafisi, contains fourteen articles by representatives of various streams of political Islam, almost all of them dealing with self-criticism and internal reform issues.

## Bibliography

### Arabic and Hebrew

Abd al-Raziq, A. (1963) *al-islam wa-usul al-hukm* ('Islam and the principles of government'), Cairo.

al-Afghani, G.A. (1986) 'al-arabiyah lesan hal al-islam wa'l-muslamin' ('Arabic, the language of Islam and the Muslims'), *Hawar*, No. 2.

Amara, M. (1985) *The Awakening of Islam and the Cultural Challenge* (in Arabic), Cairo.

Arkoun, M. (1990) *Islam, Morals, Politics* (trans. into Arabic by Hashem Saleh), Beirut.

al-Asmawi, M.S. (1987) *al-islam al-siyassi* ('Political Islam'), Cairo.

al-Banna, H. (1965) *majmu'at rasa'il al-imam al-shahid* ('Selected letters'), Beirut.

—— (n.d.) *mudhakkirat al-da'wah wa-al-da'Tyah*, Cairo: Dar al-Sehab.

al-Bishri, T. (1981) 'al-qawmiyah al-'arabiyah wa-al-islam' ('Arab nationalism and Islam'), *Al-Mustaqbal al-Arabi* ('The Arab future'), No. 26.

—— (1989) 'The General Characteristics of Islamic Thought in Modern History' (in Arabic), in al-Nafisi (1989).

Eran, G. (1985) *The Land of Israel between Religion and Politics* (in Hebrew), Jerusalem.

Fudah, F. (1988) *al-haqiqah al-gha'ibah* ('The hidden truth'), Cairo.

Hawa, S. (1979) *min ajal khatwah ila al-aman* ('For one step forward').

Ibn Hanbal, A. (n.d) *al-musnad*, Beirut.

al-Jabiri, M. (1987) 'The Problematics of Modernity and Originality', in *Heritage and the Challenge of the Age* (Symposium of the Research Centre of Arab Unity) (in Arabic), Beirut.

al-Jabiri, M. and Hanafi, H. (1990) *The Debate of the Mashreq and Maghreb* (in Arabic), Casablanca.

Kimmerling, B. (1990) 'The Strangling Noose of Zionism' (in Hebrew), *Ha'aretz*, 29 April.

Kook, A.I. (5723) (1963) *Orot ha-Qodesh* ('Lights of sanctity'), Jerusalem: Mossad Harav Kook.

Kook, Z.Y. (5727) (1967) *Li'netivot Yisrael* ('The paths of Israel'), Jerusalem: Mossad Harav Kook.

Landau, S.Z. and Y. Rabinowitz (eds), (1977) *The Book of Religious Zionism* (in Hebrew), Jerusalem.

Leibowitz, Y. (5742) (1982) *Historical Faith and Values* (in Hebrew), Jerusalem.

al-Nafisi, A. (ed.) (1989) *al-harakah al-islamiyah ru'yah mustaqbaliyah* ('The Islamic movement, a look into the future'), Cairo.

Qutb, S. (1982) *mu'alim fi al-taria* ('Stones along the way'), Cairo: Dar al-Suruq.

Ra'anan, Z. (1980) *Gush Emunim* (Hebrew), Tel Aviv: Hashomer Hatzair.

al-Reis, M. (1966) *al-nazariyah al-siyasah al-islamiyah* ('Islamic political theory'), Cairo.

Rubinstein, A. (1980) *The Land of Israel between Religion and Politics* (in Hebrew), Tel Aviv.

Schach, E.M. (1980) *Letters and Essays* (in Hebrew), Bnei Braq.

al-Senhori, A.R. (1929) 'al-din wa-al-dawlah fi-al-islam' ('Religion and state in Islam'), *Majallat al-muhamah al-sha'riyah* (periodical on religious law), October.

Sid-Ahmed, R. (1989) *The Islamic Movements in Egypt and Iran* (in Arabic), Cairo.

Sivan, E. (1986) *Islamic Zealots* (in Hebrew), Tel Aviv.

—— (1988) *Arab Political Myths* (in Hebrew), Tel Aviv.

al-Turabi, H. (1989) 'al-bu'ad al-'alami lil-harakah al-islamiyah' ('The world dimension of the Islamic movement'), in al-Nafisi (1989).

al-Yassini, A. (1987) *al-din wa-al-dawlah fi al-mamlakah al-arabiyah al-sa'udiyah* ('Religion and state in the Saudi kingdom'), London.

### English, French, and German

Ayubi, N. (1980) 'The Political Revival of Islam: The Case of Egypt', *International Journal of Middle East Studies*, Vol. XII.

Cassirer, E. (1955) *The Myth of the State*, New York.

Crecelius, D. (1972) 'Ideological Responses of the Egyptian Ulama to Modernization', in Keddie (1972).

Fisch, H. (1978) *The Zionist Revolution*, London.

Friedmann, M. (1989) 'Israel as a Theological Dilemma', in Kimmerling (1989).

Gaerts, C. (1968) *Islam Observed*, New Haven.

Ghaussy, A.G. (1989) 'Der islamisch Fundamentalismus in der Gegenwart', in Meyer (1989).

Gilsenan, M. (1988) 'Popular Islam and the State in Contemporary Egypt', in Halliday and Alavi (1988).

Halliday, F. and H. Alavi (eds) (1988) *State and Ideology in the Middle East and Pakistan*, New York.

Hiro, D. (1989) *Islamic Fundamentalism*, London.

Horkheimer, M. (ed.) (1985) *Zur Kritik der instrumentellen Vernunft*, Frankfurt am Main.

Hourani, A. (1970) *The Islamic City*, Oxford.

Ibrahim, S.E. (1989) 'Anatomy of Egypt's Militant Islamic Groups: Methodological Note and Preliminary Findings', *International Journal of Middle East Studies*, Vol. XII.

Idalovichi, I. (1989) 'Der jüdische Fundamentalismus in Israel', in Meyer (1989).

Jedaane, F. (1990) 'Notions of the State in Contemporary Arab Writings', in G. Luciani (ed.) *The Arab State*, Berkeley and Los Angeles: University of California Press.

Keddie, R.N. (ed.) (1972) *Scholars, Saints, and Muftis: Muslim Religious Institutions in the Middle East since 1500*, Berkeley and Los Angeles.

Kimmerling, B. (ed.) (1989) *The Israeli State and Society*, New York.

Lazarus-Yafeh, H. (1988) 'Contemporary Fundamentalism in Judaism, Christianity, Islam', *The Jerusalem Quarterly*, 47 (summer).

Lewis, B. (1968) *The Middle East and the West*, London.

—— (1974) 'Politics and War', in Schacht and Bosoworth (1974).

—— (1988) *The Political Language of Islam*, Chicago: University of Chicago Press.

Loewenthal, R. (1989) 'Aufklärung und Fundamentalismus als Faktoren der Weltpolitik', in Meyer (1989)

Luhmann, N. (1982) *Funktion der Religion*, Frankfurt am Main.

Meyer, T. (1989) 'Fundamentalismus, die andere Dialektik der Aufklärung', in Meyer (1989)

—— (ed.) (1989) *Fundamentalismus in der modernen Welt*, Frankfurt am Main: Suhrkamp.

Mies, M. (1972) 'Kultur Anomie als Folge westlicher Bildung', *Die Dritte Welt*, I.

Munson, H., Jr (1988) *Islam and Revolution in the Middle East*, New Haven and London.

Ravitzky, A. (1989) 'Exile in the Holy Land: The Dilemma of Haredi Jewry', *Studies in Contemporary Jewry*, V.

Rodinson, M. (1966) *Islam et capitalisme*, Paris.

Said, E. (1978) *Orientalism*, New York.

Schacht, J. and Bosoworth, C.T. (eds) (1974) *The Legacy of Islam*, Oxford.

Schulze, R. (1988) 'Der lange Bart des Propheten', in *Kursbuch* 93: 144.

Sivan, Emmanuel (1990) *Radical Islam: Medieval Theology and Modern Politics*, New Haven and London: Yale University Press.

Smith, W. (1978) *The Meaning and End of Religion*, New York.

Tibi, B. (1985) *Der Islam und das Problem der kulturellen Bewältigung sozialen Wandels*, Frankfurt am Main.

—— (1988) *The Crisis of Modern Islam*, Utah.

# 6

# The Islamic Threat and Western Foreign Policy

*Jochen Hippler*

The Middle East is a region shaped by Islam. At the same time it is a region with considerable importance for the countries of Western Europe, the USA and Japan. The oil deposits in the Persian/Arab Gulf, its former strategic significance in 'containing' the Soviet Union on its southern flank, the Arab-Israeli conflict of the last few decades, waves of migration both from the Maghreb to France and from Turkey to Germany are some important aspects of the region. Two Gulf wars within a decade, the war in Lebanon and the kidnapping of Western citizens there, the American embassy hostage crisis in Tehran during the Shiite revolution in Iran, the repression of the Kurds and their desire for self-determination, the air-raids on Libya in 1986 and the 1991 UN resolution at the culmination of the West's conflict with Libya, are others. There is no denying the significance of this region for the West. Since the Second World War and to some extent even since the nineteenth century, the USA, Great Britain and France in particular have traditionally maintained a large and active presence in the Middle East.

Western foreign policies have not ignored and could not ignore the Middle East. Given the background of the new development and refinement of the old hostile view of 'Islam' or 'Islamic fundamentalism', we must ask to what extent Western foreign and 'security' policies (a euphemism for military policy) have determined or shaped the West's relationship with Islam, and how far they continue to do so today. Have the West's foreign affairs and defence ministers perceived 'Islam' or its so-called fundamentalist variations as a threat to European and American interests? Have they understood it as an ideological or a material challenge? Or has Islam long been considered part of the harmless 'folklore' of the region? How has the West referred to Islam? Has there been a conscious policy towards the culture, politics and society of this region? Have the journalistic and pseudo-academic perceptions of the 'Islamic threat', so prevalent in Western societies (as discussed in Chapter 1 of this book), precipitated actual government policies vis-à-vis the countries of the Middle East?

## The Ideological Starting Point

Looked at superficially, the answers to the questions above are easily found. Terrorism and hostage taking by Shiite fundamentalist groups such as Hizbollah and Islamic Jihad in Lebanon, and the occupation of the American embassy in Iran by a group of students 'at the Imam's behest' (Khomeini), were spectacular acts that moved the problem of 'Islamic fundamentalism' to the centre of our consciousness. Fears of a threat and the feeling of helplessness, symbolised by the pitiful attempt in April 1980 to free the American embassy hostages by force, were very real. But then we still had 'good' Muslims, those with whom we did good business or with whom we cooperated closely in politics. The Saudi Arabian royal family are a classic example of this: their 'fundamentalist' rule is characterised by a high degree of religious intolerance, but has nonetheless been an important mainstay of Western politics in the Middle East since the mid-1940s. This being the background, what has media reporting on the region been like? Reporting is sparse in the absence of crises or outbreaks of violence; but when a crisis awakens interest, then the reporting really takes off.

I do not want to trouble my readers with a flood of amusing or shocking quotes from the international mass media at this point. But it is surely appropriate, for the purposes of illustration, to cite some examples of reporting on foreign affairs selected at random. I shall not dwell on the rabble-rousing propaganda of the tabloid press, which is to be expected in any case, but will only look at examples of 'serious' journalism.

The widely-read news magazine *Der Spiegel*, considers it its duty not only to shock and entertain its readers with the latest scandals from Bonn, or with drugs and AIDS stories, but to occasionally delight them with assessments of foreign threats.

> Does the end of the conflict between the Eastern Bloc and the West and the rise of *unpredictable fundamentalist theocratic states* on the edge of Europe, threaten us with … a *new religious war?* Will it come to an *incalculable confrontation* with *religious zealots,* whose *medieval ways of thinking* are mainly characterised by *hatred of everything Western?*[1]

This passage alone is a case in point. In the guise of a question (the article makes it clear that the questions are only rhetorical), the threat of 'theocracy' confronts us. The context makes it clear that it cannot be about the Catholic Vatican state, which is dictatorially ruled by God's representative on earth. It is about something entirely different: 'fundamentalist' theocracies. *Der Spiegel* is worried about a threat to Europe from the Middle East.

> The continued advance of *bearded zealots* in the countries of the Maghreb, neighbouring Morocco and Tunisia, whose *aggressive slogans* recall their counterparts in the *Persian Mullah State* is apparently only a matter of time.[2]

Both these quotes present a number of the elements of the perceived Islamic threat, that Andrea Lueg has examined (see Chapter 1). What is different here is that the emotive phrases are directed outwards: Europe is threatened; and the new threat is Islam. Where clarity is concerned, *Der Spiegel* has omitted nothing.

These ways of seeing are more sharply defined and widespread in Europe than they are in the USA, although they do exist there as well, albeit in a somewhat milder form. There, too, 'militant Islamic movements' are taken to be principally 'anti-Western, anti-American and anti-Israeli', to use Judith Miller's words.[3] *Time Magazine* speaks of a 'dark side of Islam, which shows its face in violence and terrorism intended to overthrow modernizing, more secular regimes and harm the Western nations that support them'.[4]

An editorial in the magazine *US News and World Report* says:

> The Gulf War was just one paragraph in the long conflict between the West and radical Islam; the World Trade Center bombing, just a sentence. We are in for a long struggle not amenable to reasoned dialogue. We will need to nurture our own faith and resolution.[5]

This view is shared by Yossef Bodansky, who overstates it almost to the point of caricature. He believes 'The Muslim World is at a historical crossroads. It has embarked on a fateful global *Jihad* (holy war) against the West and its Judeo-Christian values. America is its primary target.'[6]

In his excellent book *The Islamic Threat*, John Esposito summarises this perception of Islam as a threat:

> According to many Western commentators, Islam and the West are on a collision course. Islam is a triple threat: political, demo-

graphic, and socio-religious ... Much as observers in the past retreated to polemics and stereotypes of Arabs, Turks, or Muslims rather than addressing the specific causes of conflict and confrontation, today we are witnessing the perpetuation or creation of a new myth. The impending confrontation between Islam and the West is presented as part of a historical pattern of Muslim belligerency and aggression.[7]

This chapter will take a critical look, not at the media or at individual political commentators, but at the relationship between Western foreign policies and the Western perception of the 'Islamic threat'. At this point of departure it should be noted that the hostile perceptions of Islam described above do not only serve journalistic egoism, or the need to entertain their readers with horror stories. They are not always accompanied by alarmist cries directed outwards but are also often 'well intentioned'. Not uncommonly, the stereotypes are for this reason 'understanding', in a supposed attempt to try and understand the 'Other' – the other culture, the other people, Islam. These attempts also aim to guide Western foreign policy. An example of this approach is Hans Bräker, Professor in Cologne and Trier and 'an active member of the Foreign Office since 1957' according to the blurb of his book. Bräker talks of the 'visions' and 'dreams' of Islam, of a new jihad, and then goes on to draw his conclusions:

The logic of Gaddafi's political thinking *is difficult to understand by Western standards.* It is directed at a utopian future, and is not specific to Libya – it is a reality of many if not all Arab countries. In other words, it still determines the political thinking and behaviour of most Arab politicians. It is taking this political *reality of irrationality and utopianism* into consideration that all policies towards Arab countries must be conceived, if they are not to end in a vacuum.[8]

This stereotyped view was discussed in Chapter 1: 'Islam' and its believers are irrational and utopian. They follow a 'logic [which] ... is difficult to understand by Western standards'. Despite all his sympathy towards 'Islam', Professor Bräker has succeeded in using a beautiful turn of phrase which in fact suggests that Muslims are really mad and therefore cannot be understood. He comes dangerously close to the epithet of 'The Madman from Baghdad', that united *Der Spiegel* and the tabloid press during the second Gulf War. Bräker, however, goes further, suggesting that this assumption of collective madness must be the point of departure for formulating

Western foreign policy towards the Middle East. How we should go about this – perhaps through an equally irrational foreign policy of our own – we are of course not told.

If one takes a closer look at Western foreign policies one could almost be relieved, for actual Western foreign policy towards the Middle East has little in common with either the feared threat and the concomitant anti-Islam hysteria characteristic of much of the media or with well-meaning theories about madness.

How is the Islamic threat evaluated in the USA? What role does it have to play in determining foreign policy towards Islamic countries? We shall come back to this later, yet it should be noted that worries about the rise of Islamic tendencies also exist in the Anglo-Saxon world.

However, before we continue to look at the West's perception of Islam and Western interests in and policies towards Islam and the Middle East, let us take a quick glance at the region itself. The complex combination of all possible problems and areas of conflict that exist there should be considered.

## A Region of Conflicts

In 1992, the former US Secretary of State James Baker saw the problems of the region thus:

> We are entering an era in which ethnic and sectarian identities could easily breed new violence and conflict ... The combination of unresolved regional conflicts, turbulent social and political changes, weapons of mass destruction, and much of the world's energy supplies makes the Middle East particularly combustible.[9]

This evaluation stands out not only for its sobriety, but also for the succinct and accurate way it draws together a number of serious problems. The 'Islam' factor, however, is only referred to indirectly, in the phrase 'ethnic and sectarian identities'.

It is true that the Middle East has potential for conflict on a variety of levels. From the smouldering war in Moroccan-occupied West Sahara to the new or not so new flashpoints of the Maghreb (Algeria, Tunisia, Libya); from Egypt's growing internal political and economic instabilities to the Palestinian problem which remains unresolved despite all diplomatic efforts; from the conflict of the Kurds striving for autonomy in Turkey, Iraq and Iran, to the as yet undigested consequences of the Gulf War in Iraq, Kuwait, Saudi Arabia and other countries; from the potentially considerable instability of the Arabian

Peninsula to the recently revived conflict between the Arab Gulf states and Iran; from the problems of the new Central Asian members of the Commonwealth of Independent States including the civil war in Tadjikistan, to the recurring battles in Afghanistan – there are plenty of political and economic crises and armed conflicts today. Yet the list is far from complete: the war and crisis in Sudan and the catastrophic intervention by foreign troops in Somalia are as seldom mentioned as Lebanon, where internal political, denominational and economic conflicts continue to clash with the interests of Israel and Syria.

Even such an extremely cursory overview of the wide belt of Islamic countries from the Maghreb to the Hindu Kush shows how justified ex-Secretary of State James Baker's comments were in stressing the region's potential for conflict.

Very generally, the reasons for conflict could be divided into the following categories:

1   Attempts to institute or maintain control over areas or peoples where geographically or ethnically/religiously, they exist 'outside' the given frontiers or outside the *in-group*. This may sound very abstract, but by it I mean the following: there are disputes about territory in or around the Western Sahara, Palestine, Kashmir, the disputed Gulf Islands, Kuwait, Cyprus and other areas. Border disputes (such as those in the Arabian Peninsula, or once again between Iraq and Kuwait) also belong to this category. Apart from this, conflicts arise from attempts to exercise control over (or in fact to shake off control from) an ethnic or religious minority. This type of conflict is of course closely linked to territorial disputes: the disputed areas are as a rule inhabited by minorities or other ethnic groups. The Kurdish question or that of the Shiites in southern Iraq or Saudi Arabia, the Kashmiris, and the Palestinians in the Occupied Territories are examples.

2   The coupling of economic problems with political erosion. Often, economic difficulties alone can be overcome or survived by a stable political leadership. And unpopular, repressive or incompetent regimes or systems of government have a relatively good chance of surviving if the economic situation is good and allows for favours to be distributed among the important groups of the population. When, however, a government or ruling elite already experiencing political difficulties has to deal with an economic crisis – or if alternatively an economic crisis leads to political paralysis or a political rift – then the situation becomes serious.

In such conditions, even a country which has been stable for years or decades can turn into a regional flashpoint in a relatively short space of time. Take Algeria for example: an old-established dictatorship steadily lost its legitimacy because its political ossification was accompanied by economic incompetence and corruption. The combination of these facts with mass unemployment and an increasing lack of prospects, particularly for young people, resulted in an explosive situation that even a military coup cannot bring under control in the long term – unless the economic crisis can be overcome. Such situations of economic and political decline usually lead to an intensified battle over distribution which continues to aggravate the situation, turning it into a battle for economic means, for jobs, money, a share of the sinking national product – and to a battle for positions in the political or administrative apparatus, a battle for power.

Both these admittedly very general types of conflict do not necessarily apply to very specific crisis situations. Whether armed or military clashes or even war or civil war will transpire, whether the degree of political polarisation in the societies concerned is the problem, or if the relevant ruling elites are divided or united against revolts 'from below', or what ideological direction an opposition movement is likely to assume – all this and much more can only be discussed by reference to the actual situation.

On the whole, however, it is apparent that the numerous interconnected problems and conflicts in the Middle East can in most cases be related to the political failure of the regimes and political elites in question. Moreover, this failure has economic dimensions (such as mass unemployment or rising prices for basic food commodities), political-psychological (the delegitimation of the elite and their ideologues), organisational (the fragmentation, corruption or incompetence of the state apparatus and its bureaucracy) and foreign dimensions (dependency on a foreign superpower).

In many Middle Eastern countries the ruling elites have long promised economic development, independence and a solution to the Palestinian problem, to mention but a few examples. Yet they have increasingly proved themselves incapable of resolving even a fraction of the problems of their countries, and instead have only pursued the interests of power, and in the process not uncommonly amply lined their own pockets. Western countries (and earlier to a certain extent the Soviet Union) have played an important contributory role in this. They have collaborated with the ruling elites, and in some cases even helped them to hold on to power artificially. Whether the various reactionary sheikhdoms in the Gulf (including

Saudi Arabia) would have continued to exist over the last few decades without the West's interest in oil is debatable at the very least. Often, there has been a community of interests between Western governments and Middle Eastern dictatorships (the region being virtually free of democracy) against the people of Middle Eastern countries.

The West (and the USSR) have for generations helped repressive and often incompetent regimes hang on to power. In this way, instead of contributing to the resolution of problems they have only helped to aggravate and perpetuate them. Internal stagnation, the failure of ruling elites and prolonged economic misery are therefore, for a lot of people in the Middle East, closely connected with the West's predominance in the region. This perception may be exaggerated at times, and may also be dressed up as a conspiracy theory, but it is essentially appropriate. It is hardly surprising then that in the long term a considerable potential for resistance would build up in the Middle East, which would be directed not only against the dictators there but also against the men behind them – the West. What would Saddam Hussein have been without Western and Soviet arms and engineers? What would the Saudi monarchy be without American protection?

We have now reached the point where we must ask questions about Western interests in foreign policies regarding the Middle East. We have very briefly mentioned several important problems of the region – but what is the West's interest there?

## The Middle East and Western Interests

The beauty of Washington's politics often lies in its openness. A superpower can afford to make its own interests crystal clear, and in the next breath confer the greater glory of morality on its politics with all manner of fine words. How then does Washington see the essence of its own Middle Eastern policies? The then director of the American military secret service, the DIA (Defense Intelligence Agency), Lieutenant General James Clapper, presented a congressional committee with an overview of the position of America's military and foreign policy interests a year after the Gulf War.

> In the Middle East, lasting regional stability will be difficult to achieve and our military intelligence effort will focus, in large part, on the resurgence of Iraqi and Iranian military power and nuclear proliferation.

Over the next 10 to 15 years, Iran and Iraq will continue their competition for hegemony in the Gulf and will seek to strengthen their military capabilities. A secular state in Iraq, and a religious state in Iran are inherently at cross purposes. This enmity is likely to lead to situations in which war is a distinct possibility. A renewal of warfare in the Gulf would once again threaten world oil supplies.[10]

The military power of other countries, the proliferation of nuclear weapons and competition between two regional powers (both hostile to the USA) that could threaten world oil supplies: these are what the most senior official of US military intelligence perceives as threats. The religious question comes up only indirectly here – within the framework of the rivalry between Iran and Iraq – and apparently it is not of such great significance that the USA would automatically support the secular Iraqi dictatorship against the religiously legitimised Iranian one. There is a marked sobriety and pragmatism about the words quoted above, as there is in Clapper's entire position.

Yet his viewpoint is by no means exceptional but entirely typical of the politics of the US government. What are made particularly clear are American interests (which in this case overlap with those of Western Europe) as regards the second Gulf War. At that time, US Defense Secretary Cheney also defined his country's interests in the Gulf, especially where Iraq was concerned:

Failure to counter Iraq's aggression and territorial gains would have severe consequences for U.S. interests. In the short term, Iraq could manipulate and cause destabilizing uncertainty in the international oil market, force up prices to crippling levels, threaten regional states, and begin the process of building a strong and widespread political base. With the conquest of Kuwait, Saddam Hussein has direct control of the capacity to produce five million barrels of oil a day and a potentially strong influence over production of the rest of the Arabian Peninsula, which is another seven million barrels a day. This would give Saddam Hussein an extremely powerful oil weapon. With this weapon, he could coerce oil importing nations in Europe, Japan, and even the United States, which depend increasingly on Gulf oil.

Over the long term, Iraq would be much stronger militarily. Given its additional resources, Iraq could expand its vast arsenal of conventional and non-conventional weaponry – soon to include nuclear weapons. His military strength, coupled with enhanced economic and political power, would give Saddam Hussein even greater coercive power over his neighbors on oil and other issues.[11]

Whether this viewpoint was right or wrong is not a question of debate here. We are concerned not with examining Western energy policies in the Gulf, but with looking at the connection between the West's foreign policies and certain ideological patterns. And here, Cheney presents us with a markedly unideological, materialistic definition of interests: Saddam would represent a threat for the USA – and the whole of the West – because:

1 Iraq would raise oil prices significantly
2 the West could be coerced by Iraq's 'oil weapon'
3 Iraq would gain increased military power in the region.

Secretary Baker had defined the economic standpoint even more clearly. In this connection there have always been misunderstandings between the right and the left: as if 'the oil supply could have been cut off' or as if the Gulf War had primarily been about regulating oil prices. 'No Blood for Oil', the short and catchy slogan used by sections of the peace movement, was an example of this misunderstanding. Baker, by contrast, made it clear:

and perhaps most obviously, what is at stake economically is the dependence of the world on access to the energy resources of the Persian Gulf. The effects on our economy and our people are already being felt. But this is not about increases in the price of a gallon of gas at your local service station. It is not just a narrow question of the flow of oil from Kuwait and Iraq. It is about a dictator who, acting alone and unchallenged, could strangle the global economic order, determining by fiat whether we all enter a recession or even the darkness of a depression.[12]

Western interests in the Persian Gulf naturally revolve around oil and energy supplies. Yet it is not a question of the mere economic variables of the amount and price of oil exports. It is a question of power, a question of controlling the oil-producing region and of keeping this control from others – especially those of unfriendly disposition. Many other interests are subordinate to this aim, but the Middle East is not only made up of the Gulf region, and Western interests are correspondingly more complex. In her article on Persian Gulf security, Shireen Hunter retrospectively summarised the threats the West and particularly the USA perceived as coming from the Middle East, until the end of the 1980s. 'Traditionally the principal threats to regional security have stemmed from Soviet expansionism and regional radicalism.'[13] Building on this, Hunter goes on to name six categories of threat to Western interests, among which are:

- oil as a political weapon
- the threat to conservative Arab rulers sympathetic to the West
- the perception of Israel's interests as an ally of the West in the region
- regional rivalries between states or movements that could lead to instability
- internal political and economic problems of individual countries in the region.[14]

During the Cold War, all these threats to Western interests were naturally related to the rivalry with the Soviet Union. A further point in Hunter's list (although she puts it in fourth place) concerns ideological questions and touches on our theme directly. It is about the threat to Western interests from Islam and Arab nationalism:

the views of militant Islamists and radical Arab nationalists on the nature of the governments and ruling elites of the Persian Gulf Arab states are quite similar. The two groups also share an animosity toward the West. However, unlike Arab Nationalists, the Islamists, with few exceptions, were also anti-Soviet.[15]

What Hunter considers to be Western foreign policy fears about 'militant Islam' boil down to the fact that it is focused against the West. It is hardly surprising that the West does not cherish such an attitude. Nevertheless, it is clear that even militant Islam – that is to say, Islamic movements – was considered somewhat *less* hostile than Arab nationalism (of the Nasserite or Ba'athist kind) because it was also anti-Soviet; and in times of acute rivalry between the Western and Eastern blocs, the position regarding the Soviet Union was the decisive criterion in distinguishing friend from foe. The 'Islamic' threat so popular in much of the mass media is placed here as one of six threats, and only as a half threat: it is seen as a subgenus of hostile ideologies and in fact as the less dangerous one.

## Communism and Islam

Unfriendly powers are to be kept under control as far as possible and kept out of the strategically important oil regions. This view is not new, it stems from the early days of the Cold War and is still current.

In the past, when Western policy makers and strategists considered the Persian/Arab Gulf or the Middle East as a whole, their prime concern was the Soviet threat, not Islam. Almost all other factors were evaluated within this context.

As such, Islam, even in its militant variations, seemed rather harmless to the West's political elite. It could become important, however, if Islamist tendencies were to exert a negative influence on the other five vital Western interests, i.e. the oil question, the stability of pro-Western regimes, the Western partner Israel, and internal political or regional instabilities in which Islam would assume an increasingly threatening and aggressive role. Then and only then would Islam become a problem for Western foreign ministries, and it would be irrelevant which variations or interpretations of Islam were involved. Therefore, it was not religious character, nor cultural tradition nor Islam that was a problem for Western foreign policy, but actions which threatened Western interests. Regardless of whether these stemmed from religious or secular sources, anti-Western policies could not be tolerated, especially in times of conflict between the West and the Eastern bloc as any anti-Western policy could easily be of advantage to Eastern Europe.

Indeed it has long been the case that the West has used Islam as a weapon against communism. Islam was often considered a conservative ideology that could be used to resist revolutionary communist ideologies or even Arab nationalism. Anderson and Rashidian say as much, looking at the CENTO pact of the 1950s, which, with the cooperation of the governments in question, was supposed to mobilise a belt of conservative Islamic countries against the Soviet Union. This idea failed, however, as a result of the nationalist revolution in Iraq. The authors go on to look at another quite significant case:

> The ideal result of a Khomeini Regime would be a fundamentalist 'curtain', fulfilling more effectively the role once undertaken by CENTO. With 50 million Muslim citizens in its south-central states, any Soviet moves beyond its borders in the region would be likely to encounter the full wrath of Islam ... Thus, ... however [Khomeini's] regime came into being, the effect was to place a blockage upon any substantial Soviet movement.[16]

This idea is surprising but at the same time obvious. Despite all the anti-Western militancy of the early phase of the Islamic revolution in Iran, it would still guarantee that any advance by the Soviet Union in the proximity of the Persian Gulf would be fiercely resisted. And we must not forget that especially following the Soviet intervention in Afghanistan (at the end of 1979), US policy makers continued to reckon with further incursions as far as the Gulf. However, it must be pointed out here that despite this fact, Khomeini's accession to power and the subsequent developments were in no way in the interests of the USA. What they gained in fencing off the Soviet Union was lost in terms of their own influence in the region.

The partial conflict of interests with Islamist powers was not, however, limited to individual cases or historical coincidence. From the 1970s till well into the 1980s the Israeli government fostered the Muslim Brotherhood (and its offshoot, Hamas)[17] in the Occupied Territories – the same group that was later considered to be especially dangerous. The American magazine *Newsweek* explained it thus:

> For years the Arab fundamentalists seemed like dependable pawns in a series of high-stakes proxy battles. They bitterly opposed the West's main enemies – communism and its regional allies, left-wing Arab nationalists. Hostile to the Palestine Liberation Organization, they seemed perfect for an Israeli divide-and-conquer strategy. And they were theologically in tune with the West's key Arab ally and oil supplier, Saudi Arabia ... In the 1970s, [Israel] began building up the Brotherhood as a counterbalance to the PLO – and continued even after Israeli troops began battling Shiite radicals in Lebanon.[18]

During the 1980s, there was another instance of long and systematic cooperation with Islamist groups against the Soviet Union: with the Afghan Mujahidin (the conflict with Shiite Iran on the other hand became more acute despite its anti-Soviet position). Support of the Mujahidin with goods and arms against the Soviet troops and, following the Soviet withdrawal, against the secular (and by virtue of collaboration with the Soviet Union, discredited) regime of President Najibullah, was the largest and most successful operation by the CIA, the American secret service abroad. The Mujahidin received approximately $3.5 billion in arms and other aid from the CIA, regardless of their political orientation or Islamist zeal.[19] In this way, the most radical Islamist group – Gulbuddin Hekmatyar's party – received two-thirds of American aid over two years. Yet for a long time, it did not seem to worry the CIA that Hekmatyar's party was openly not only anti-Soviet but also anti-American, and that it was responsible for massacres, torture and just about every conceivable human rights abuse, quite apart from the fact that Hekmatyar was also trafficking in heroin on the side. If there is such a thing as the classic fundamentalist leader, straight out of Western stories, then it is Hekmatyar. Despite this Washington had no reservations, but only arms and money to offer. After all, the enemy of my enemy is my friend. Of all the Afghan Mujahidin groups, his was the best organised and militarily most powerful – the natural partner for an anti-Soviet campaign. It was only some time after the USSR had withdrawn from Afghanistan, in fact only when the USA and the Soviet Union cooperated closely in the run-up to the Gulf War of 1990–1 that the USA distanced itself from Hekmatyar's party. It was certainly no coincidence that this occurred at a time when the fundamentalist leader openly took Saddam Hussein's side in the Gulf conflict. It was only then that the Americans acknowledged his well-known crimes, reduced their support for him and finally ended it.

When Najibullah's government collapsed as a result of internal strife (April 1992), it once again became clear which factions the USA and the West had supported for more than a decade. The civil war was not at an end; in Kabul it had only just begun. The freedom fighters vociferously celebrated by the West for years descended upon each other with their weapons, tyrannised the population and battled on the streets. The success of the great CIA operation had served the USA in inflicting defeat on the Soviet Union; but it had damaged Afghanistan almost as much as the Soviet occupation. Hekmatyar became the prime minister, and the fighting in and around Kabul became bloodier and more protracted than ever.

Western policies towards Pakistan were similar. From 1977 to 1978 Pakistan was ruled by Zia ul-Haq, an Islamist general who had come to power through a military coup. In the 1980s the USA gave massive support and arms to this military ruler – they needed his country as a base from which to support the Mujahidin against the Soviet Union in the war in Afghanistan. The building of a Pakistani atom bomb, the involvement of his dictatorship in heroin smuggling to Europe and other activities were looked upon as mere peccadilloes and generously ignored – to say nothing of the repression of the Pakistani people and widespread human rights abuse. On Zia's death the secular members of the Washington government surpassed themselves in their eulogies.

Reagan, in a written statement issued from his ranch near Santa Barbara, recalled his meetings with Zia, saying they had 'worked together for peace and stability' ... The Pakistani leader, the statements said, 'also believed in freedom for Afghanistan' ... Vice President Bush ... told reporters that 'Pakistan and the United States have a very special relationship, and the loss of General Zia is a great tragedy'.[20]

The fact that this dictator had followed an Islamist fundamentalist programme in order to widen his political base, and had fostered Islamist parties on a massive scale, presented no problem. The reason: the USA needed Pakistan as a base of operations for the war in Afghanistan.

Another example of flexible dealings with Islamist regimes is of course Saudi Arabia. The power system in this country is characterised by a high degree of religious intolerance, even greater than in Iran. In Iran, Christians and Jews have their own seats in parliament – in Saudi Arabia it is forbidden to build a church. If there is such a thing as a fossilised fundamentalist state, then it is Saudi Arabia. The country's elite cultivates practices which in other circumstances the West would find highly objectionable. For example, as far back as the 1970s its religious leaders sentenced a foreign dissident to death. However, it was not a man with a Western passport like Salman Rushdie, but a rather unpopular personality in the West: Muammar Gaddafi. The Saudi leadership has also traditionally been committed to exporting its own model of fundamentalism. The Islamists in Sudan and other countries have been nurtured with Saudi money. Even an anti-Israeli and, worse, an anti-Semitic orientation in Saudi politics were not taken amiss by Washington, London and Bonn. The country is after all firmly in the Western camp. Religious nonsense is a private matter for its rulers. It was hardly surprising, then, that the secular West militarily defended fundamentalist Saudi Arabia against secular Iraq. As far as the Gulf is concerned, it is not religion that matters so much as power and strategic interests. Pro-Western fundamentalists are considerably better than a nationalistic technocratic regime that the West cannot control. Even *Newsweek* noticed this much:

> The United States, Britain, France, Saudi Arabia, Kuwait – and Israel itself – all have a long history of complex ties with Islamic groups now denounced as 'terrorists' ... Western nations had nothing against extremism, so long as it was channelled in the right direction.[21]

Of course this is not the whole picture. In Washington and London, and to a lesser extent in Paris, they have repeatedly tried to use Islam and even Islamic fundamentalism for their own purposes, usually against the Soviet Union and communism. If you wanted to fight Marxist-Leninist ideology, it was practical to oppose it with another all-encompassing ideology. Just as Protestant sects were used in the fight against Marxism and liberation theology in Central

America, wherever possible Islam has been used to fight secular Arab nationalism/socialism and communism.

In the 1970s and 1980s, the perception of Islam or Islamism as hostile was softened by the joint opposition of the West and some Islamic countries towards the Soviet Union and communism. Islamism was either a 'lesser evil' or actually very useful. This has changed completely since the end of the Cold War. Our perception of Islam can no longer be moderated by the existence of an even worse ideological opponent. Neither communism nor Arab nationalism poses a serious threat to Western interests today. As a result, Islam or Islamism is moving into the firing line, and in fact often replacing the old enemy. In conversation, a German lieutenant colonel casually put it like this: 'Islam is the new communism.'

What is new, following the end of the Cold War, is the tendency in the West to build up Islam as the dangerous ideological successor to Marxism-Leninism. In an article in the *New York Times Magazine*, Judith Miller points out with characteristic accuracy:

> The west tends to regard the growing political popularity of Islam as dangerous, monolithic and novel ... The rise of militant Islam has triggered a fierce debate about what, if anything, the West can or should do about it. Some American officials and commentators have already designated militant Islam as the west's new enemy, to be 'contained' much the way communism was during the cold war.[22]

Such views are not restricted to the USA. One is sometimes given the impression that Islam is the ideological successor to Marxism-Leninism, resembling its predecessor in almost every aspect. In the German weekly *Das Parlament* (which at times manages to reach new heights of boredom in its seriousness), an unspeakable article appearing on the first anniversary of the Gulf War ('The Threat to Europe by Islamic Radicalism') sums up this tendency: 'The new totalitarian idea: Islamic Fundamentalism.'[23]

I do not want to dwell on the subject in order to establish that neither Islam nor its fundamentalist variations are *new*, as the ingenious author of the article in *Das Parlament* would have us believe. Yet we must ask why it is only *now* that an old matter has been rediscovered and interpreted as the totalitarian counter-alternative to the West. Surely this has more to do with an ideological lacuna in Western identity and its need to be filled after the Cold War, than it does with the matter under consideration. It is hardly surprising, then, that the same author should use a well-worn phrase from earlier days in order to use Islam as a counterpoint to European self-definition: Islam and its radicalism on the one hand and *'the free world'* on the other.[24] Until recently this phrase was still used to demarcate the alternatives – freedom or communism.

## The Islamic Threat

Strange as it may be, in the practical politics of Western countries it often seems as if the view of Islam as a threat does not exist or only plays a subordinate role. Excited ideologues debate foreign policies and have ample suggestions to offer, but are not really taken seriously. Everyday politics gives the impression of being 'pragmatic', if not opportunistic. There are good and bad fundamentalists, our Islamists and the others. Yet the situation is not really quite like this. Even in foreign affairs, there is also an element of seeing Islam – or its fundamentalist variations – as a threat to the West.

Terrorism has a central place in this ideology. There are two ways of dealing with this problem, and they are interrelated. Again, one has its origins in the way of thinking characteristic of the Cold War. An example is a statement by Fred Iklé (the then Secretary of State for Political Affairs in the US Defense Department) made on the occasion of a Senate hearing in May 1985 where he spoke of two sources of terrorism: 'At present, there are two ideologies that foster terrorism: communism and some forms of Islamic fundamentalism, mostly from Iran and Libya.'[25]

Here communism and Islamism are equated as threats and it is their common anti-Western orientation and potential for violence that is considered. This view sees Middle Eastern terrorism as a threat to the West and only marginally as a religious matter. There is also another perspective.

> To put it briefly: Shiite terrorism 'couples' the Koran with the Kalashnikov. *Terror and mosque are closely linked.* And considering the almost incomprehensible spiritual energy of these phenomena, as far as we West Europeans today are concerned, an effective way of combating such a form of terrorism is extremely difficult, if not in the final analysis even impossible.[26]

This evaluation came from Rolf Tophoven of the Institute for Terrorism Research (Institut für Terrorismusforschung) in Bonn, an institution which apparently has good contacts in the secret services. Here, Shiite terrorism is described as a mainly religious affair, for after all 'terror and mosque are closely linked'. Counter-measures are so difficult because of the 'incomprehensible spiritual energy' of this connection. Conceptually these two statements are somewhat at variance, but this is of little practical relevance since this pseudo-religious explanation of Middle Eastern terrorism is mainly conveyed by the old guard of anti-communists, and is switched back and forth between points flexibly and at will. The details are unimportant as long as the image of the 'enemy' is clearly drawn. Tophoven, the expert on terrorism, explains the connection:

> When, on coming to power, Ayatollah Khomeini proclaimed Holy War, Muslims all over the world were electrified. This Holy War was aimed at the West, and its instruments were the terror personified in the commandos of the fanatical warriors of God, Hizbollah. Ever since, a prairie fire has been raging: Islamic fanatics are taking a stand against the threatened modernisation and westernisation ... The extensive Shiite fire laid by Khomeini has long since spread to the Sunnis, the largest religious group in Islam.[27]

In other words the West is threatened by a terrorist holy war originally of Shiite orientation, now of Sunni orientation as well. This quote is a very good example of the way the perception of an Islamic threat has developed in foreign affairs. What is interesting, however, is the fact that Khomeini (a reactionary fanatic for whom any sympathy would be superfluous) never declared a 'holy war against the West', in contrast to the secular Saddam Hussein whose theologically easygoing nature was susceptible to the idea of jihad.[28]

Khomeini did indeed use the word 'jihad' on many occasions, but very carefully, in the traditional Shiite sense of the individual's striving for and commitment to fighting corruption, repression, exploitation and other social evils. Even if the Ayatollah was unpopular, and rightly so, he never did call for a holy terrorist war against the West.[29]

But these are apparently details that should not confuse or blur our clear image of 'the enemy'. It is after all a question of defining our own perception of threat and naming the enemy not one of understanding him or wanting to know something about him. For it is we who are affected and not our foreign political partner:

> Middle Eastern terrorist groups and politically and religiously motivated fanatics do not only see Israel and the USA as their enemies but also the European countries allied to them. Consequently, the operative playing field of international terrorism in

the 1990s could increasingly extend to Europe. Germany is in particular danger of turning into 'the battleground of international terrorism from a region of operation' (Horchem).'[30]

This of course begs the question of how exactly someone like Tophoven expects the West to be protected from the terrorist threats of fanatical Shiites. But he has a solution ready. With some sense of surprise we read the following:

> In the long term the Shiite terrorists can only be contained, at least partially, by targeting *the state* on which they depend for support. Diplomatic pressure applied equally by Western and Eastern Europe, and economic sanctions would dampen the fanaticism of the mullahs in Tehran as well as the Greater Syrian ambitions in Damascus. In the past, these principles of fighting terrorism have partially worked repeatedly and have to some extent been successful.[31]

The helplessness is almost touching – the expert has fallen into his own trap. He first constructs a threat posed by unpredictable religious fanatics who are completely alien to Western logic. Then, the pragmatist in him forces him to suggest solutions (whether he wants to or not); and the solutions he draws from the hat are 'diplomatic pressure' and 'economic sanctions' – measures that could hardly have any effect if the opponents were really as irrational, fanatical or unpredictable as he earlier made them out to be. 'Diplomatic pressure' – would that really make an impression on *Der Spiegel*'s 'bearded zealots'? Tophoven himself appears to have noticed this paradox as he has punctuated his policy suggestions with qualifying adjectives: ('partially', yet at the same time 'repeatedly' – what next?) and he only expects success 'to some extent'. Partial successes to some extent, then, are what Tophoven hopes for. This may be realistic, but his cautious expressions contrast sharply with the strong language he has otherwise used for his fables on Islam and the Shiites.

We have reached an important point here. Those like Tophoven and his Anglo-Saxon colleagues[32] who like to regard the people, political movements and governments of the Middle East as irrational and incapable of understanding 'Western logic' rob themselves of any possibility of a successful policy vis-à-vis the region. With this attitude neither equal cooperation nor 'diplomatic pressure' is realistic. Theoretically, the only options left are complete dissociation from the madmen – or the use of force, either the manipulative force of a psychiatrist or that of a coloniser. What is presented to us here as so enlightenedly critical of religion (i.e. critical of Islam and fundamentalism) is in fact marked by a return to pre-Enlightenment politics and thought. The talk is no longer of interests, but about religion, and often without any real knowledge of the subject. Or, on the basis of speculation and assumption, the Other is attributed with qualities which question his/her rationality. Finally one comes to a point where there is no place for rational policies, where politics and their stated aims no longer match. The supposed irrationality of the Other becomes the basis for our own politics.

## The Islamic Atom Bomb

Another focal point of Western fears is the 'Islamic bomb'. In its broader and more updated version, this threat has come to include all forms of weapons of mass destruction (ABC – atomic, biological and chemical – weapons) and carrier systems, such as missiles. The threat is still considered to come mainly from dictatorial regimes and Islam or its fundamentalist variations. Depending on the economic situation, fear of the Islamic bomb works in phases focusing on this or that country: Libya, Pakistan, Algeria, Iraq, Iran and more recently on some of the Central Asian republics of the former Soviet Union. Occasionally, even serious publications foresee Iran or some other Muslim country installing missiles targeting Western Europe in Albania – 'half-way between Baghdad and Berlin'.[33]

It goes without saying that the spread of weapons of mass destruction and missile technology is a particularly serious political problem. These weapons systems should be reduced in number, and ultimately abolished. It is particularly dangerous if nuclear weapons are introduced, produced or stockpiled in a region as unstable and rife with conflict as the Middle East. (Similarly, the preceding arguments do not minimise the dreadfulness of terrorist attacks.) But we are concerned with quite a different question here – two questions in fact: first, from a Western perspective, exactly what is it that constitutes the threat? Since a number of Western regimes have weapons of mass destruction at their disposal, it can hardly be their existence as such. Second, what does the question about weapons of mass destruction have to do with Islam? How does religion come into play here? Is a Hindu or Christian/Jewish bomb somehow basically different?

Let us begin with the second point, as it will anyway lead us back to the first point. The *New York Times* recently looked at the question of the threatening 'Islamic wave'. Among other things, Judith Miller's article 'The Islamic Wave' looked at the rise of the fundamentalist

Islamic Salvation Front (FIS) in Algeria. From a discussion with a Western diplomat, she quotes: 'Algeria has a nuclear program, which it vows is for peaceful purposes. "Imagine not just the restoration of the Islamic caliph, a leader who combines temporal and spiritual power," the diplomat says, "but a nuclearized caliph".'[34]

In addition to the problem of the non-proliferation of nuclear weapons, we have the problem of Islamist control of these weapons. This is hardly surprising: if you assume a culture and region, and its population, political movements and governments to be irrational, unpredictable and blindly fanatic, then of course they should not come to possess such dangerous weapons. Conversely, from the Western perspective, there is something comforting in this assumption: the fact that until now (Western) nuclear weapons have never been deployed for military purposes – apart from two deplorable exceptions – is further proof of the rationality and level-headedness of the West. Thus, Western rationality is a licence for the possession of nuclear weapons; and at the same time implies a claim to rationality and its *Western* character – in contrast to the other irrational opponent. Western and rational – the words are a pleonasm.

Only some months before the Gulf War, an Iraqi diplomat accused the West of double standards as regards weapons of mass destruction. While American, French and Israeli nuclear bombs are seen as securing peace, Arab C-weapons are opposed:

> Developments in the field of military research are closely connected to our aim of creating scientific and technological capabilities, in all areas. The Arabs or Iraq are not forbidden to build laboratories and carry out research. And why should they be? Why should you assume that Israel would only use its chemical weapons sensibly and responsibly, while the Arabs would shoot around with theirs? This is racist and unrealistic.[35]

Obviously this was meant to justify the Iraqi military build-up. But the Iraqi government representative was using a reasonable argument for the wrong purpose – that atomic weapons are totally acceptable in the hands of the European powers or South Africa and Israel, and that this situation is at worst uncomfortable, whereas an 'Islamic bomb' would be something of a political catastrophe. Conversely, this ethnocentric-racist core of the Western argument and fear functions in exactly the same way as the Iraqi argument: here a false argument is used for a desirable aim, nuclear disarmament. This is well and good, but the West has only the disarmament of *the Other* in mind, not its own.

We should not forget that this juxtaposition of our own 'rational' handling of the bomb with the irresponsible striving of the Other for the same weapon is aimed at concealing our own Achilles heel. This argument after all, depends on our own rationality. Yet the problem is that Western (and Soviet) nuclear weapons policies of the last fifty years can hardly be described as 'rational'. Without going into details here, the strategy of *mutual assured destruction* can only be described as what its acronym so accurately spells: MAD. The whole gamut of atomic war strategies and related doctrines developed from the Second World War onwards, including such notions as *flexible response* or *forward defence* had more to do with nuclear theology than with rational policy planning. Both sides had to *believe* in them in order for them to function – regardless of their nonsensical basis. Even the firm belief that 'our weapons are good and further the cause of peace, while yours are bad and threaten it' only works on the level of power politics, not of rationality. It is a myth, the myth that even the work of the devil is good as long as it is only in our hands.

The absurdity and irrationality of the Western argument also becomes clear if one considers particularly the arms trade as a whole and the aid given for missile and ABC weapons production in the Middle East. Thus, the *supply* of modern conventional weapons and those of mass destruction to the Middle East by Western countries and firms is considered rational in terms of politics or economic trade, or just possibly a trivial offence. Yet the *purchase* of the self-same weapons systems by Middle Eastern clients is seen as criminal, as an expression of megalomania and Middle Eastern unpredictability.

Clearly, the spread of weapons of mass destruction in the Middle East and the rest of the world has little to do with ideological or religious questions and a great deal to do with power. As so often we obtain the best information on this state of affairs from officials in Washington. Almost eight months before the Iraqi occupation of Kuwait, a senior official from the US Defense Department explained the problem:

A ... second key fact is that we are facing a world in which *military power has come into the hands of a widening circle of states, all of whom reserve the right to use it as they see fit.* You are all familiar with our concern over the proliferation of ballistic missiles, chemical weapons, and the technology to produce nuclear weapons. It is not less important that many states in the so-called Third World have highly advanced conventional weapons such as cruise missiles, and have them in quantity. The Iraqi army's tank fleet, for instance, is comparable in size to that of the Bundeswehr. *Potential adver-*

*saries in the Third World are no longer trivial military problems*, if indeed they ever were: Grenada is not the kind of conflict we are likely to see often, nor is it the challenge against which we should measure our requirements.[36]

There are no ideological finger exercises here: 'Islam' is not endowed with anything unknown to us or that we do not practise ourselves. It is a question of power politics, of control. The problem is the growing military power of 'many states in the so-called Third World', who could thereby escape Western dominance. The problem is that 'a widening circle of states reserve the right' to use their power 'as they see fit': a dreadful nightmare for power politicians, a banality in international law, commonly known as national sovereignty. The alternative is of course that the countries in question should behave in a manner that *other* countries 'see fit' and not as they themselves 'see fit'.

In February 1990, President Bush announced that a most urgent problem was that 'inevitably high-tech weapons will fall into the hands of those whose hatred of America, and contempt for civilized norms, is well-known. We will continue to work hard to prevent *this* dangerous proliferation'.[37] It is not a question, then, of the abolition or reduction of weapons of mass destruction or extensive disarmament, but one of keeping from one's opponents weapons systems that could enhance their power. And these are of course weapons of mass destruction, missile technology, every high-tech or 'intelligent' weapons system, or any effective form of armament. What is important is that we – the West – strengthen ourselves, that we defend, fortify and establish our own supremacy, and monopolise the most effective and dangerous weapons systems as far as possible. Practically speaking this often simply means enhancing American power. In this process, two categories of states are treated somewhat more leniently, but for different reasons: political friends and allies (such as Great Britain and Israel) on the one hand and other atomic powers that already exist (such as the former Soviet Union or today's Russia, the People's Republic of China and India) on the other. In the first case it is friendship and mutual interests, in the second realism and the acknowledgement of the inevitable, that dampen the possibility of conflict.

In this respect, the danger of an 'Islamic bomb' is predominantly the danger of countries from the Third World breaking out of the Western-dominated system of international relations. We have now come full circle. Islam is not a problem as such, nor is it a threat in itself, even ideologically. But Islam can work as a pro-Western or anti-

Western force. This is even true of 'Islamic fundamentalism'. However, the situation becomes really serious when anti-Western feelings run high. When these feelings are expressed in Islamic categories, when the anti-Western position has a religious basis, then fear of Islam seems appropriate, just as was the case earlier with Arab nationalism. The fear, then, is one of anti-Western sentiments and politics, however these may be expressed.

Shireen Hunter has got to the heart of the matter; it is not for any spiritual reasons that the West fears fundamentalism, but rather for very concrete reasons: 'However, Islamic sentiments are still strong in the region. The fundamentalists are particularly averse to a permanent, large-scale presence of foreign military forces in Muslim lands.'[38]

If the Islamic fundamentalists were pro-Western, if they would support American military bases in the Middle East and keep oil prices reasonable and stable, what could we then have against Islamic fundamentalism?

## Politics, Religion and Foreign Affairs

President George Bush used to conclude his important speeches by proclaiming: 'God bless you. God bless our beloved country.' Towards the end of his term he even ascribed the end of the Cold War not only to his own competence, but also to the supernatural. 'By the grace of God, America won the Cold War.'[39] He elevated the Gulf War and the conflict with Saddam Hussein to a religious level in the same way: it had been a 'crusade'. He had always known that 'God' was 'on our side'.[40] Despite the official separation of state and religion in the USA (and a few other Western countries) this was not a case of isolated slips of the tongue. Bill Clinton followed this custom right from the beginning: even in his inaugural speech he beseeched God's help to guide him in his office, and God's blessings for his land. Such religious incantations from the highest office in the government have a long tradition in the USA, secular state or not. As early as 1898, President McKinley recounted how he had come to the decision to annex the Philippines. 'I walked the floor of the White House night after night until midnight, went down on my knees and prayed Almighty God for light and guidance.' One night he received God's answer: there was no question of leaving the Philippines to America's rivals France or Germany, or of leaving them to themselves. McKinley continued:

there was nothing left for us to do but to take them all, and to educate the Filipinos, and uplift and civilize and Christianize them and by God's grace [which would later win the Cold War] do the very best we could by them, as our fellow men for whom Christ has also died. And then I went to bed, and to sleep, and slept soundly.[41]

Inspiration from God as the basis for foreign policies and colonial expansion – should we use this as an argument to question the secular nature of the USA or Western societies as a whole? Where does 'Western rationality' stand in such instances? In his efforts to reach an agreement between Israel and Egypt at Camp David, President Carter often liked to bring God into the picture. 'I think the fact that we worship the same God and are bound by basically the same moral principles is a possible source for resolution of differences. I was always convinced that if Sadat and Begin could get together, they would be bound by that common belief.'[42]

Here Islam does not appear to be a threat; the common ground between Islam, Judaism and Christianity is seen as a precondition of the Camp David Agreement. Should we take this seriously? Are such examples or other countless and equally bizarre ones from the Reagan administration indicative of the religious nature of Western politics? Probably not. But they do arouse justified doubts about the comfortable pair of opposites – Western/secular/rational on the one hand, and Middle Eastern/Islamic/religious/irrational on the other. We should remind ourselves that big words uttered by politicians should not automatically be taken at face value, but are often used simply to legitimise their actions. Obvious as that may appear to us where our own cultural area is concerned, we do tend to take the religious utterances of other cultures literally – as if they were not political pronouncements but actual religious ones.

Let us change the perspective. Terrible and threatening things are indeed taking place in the Middle East. There are instances of one country striving for dominance over another, and of course the dangers of terrorism and the proliferation of weapons of mass destruction mentioned above do exist. Moreover, the Middle East is a region where political statements are couched in religious or quasi-religious language, much stronger than that used by Washington. A worldly and Arab nationalist dictator such as Saddam Hussein considers it appropriate to interpret his conflict with the USA and its allies in religious terms and to call for a holy war. Of course our criticism of the West's construction of the Islamic threat does not necessarily mean that fanaticism or religious dogmatism do not exist in the Middle

East. We are after all critical of the same manifestations in our own cultural area.

It would, however, be absurd to want to explain the real and dangerous aspects of Middle Eastern society and politics on the basis of religious phenomena. Let us take the example of Iranian foreign policy and Professor Bassam Tibi, a Middle East expert well known in Europe and the USA. In 1992, an article by Professor Tibi, entitled 'Concealing Foreign Policy', was published in the *Frankfurter Allgemeine Zeitung*.[43] The pattern of argument in this article is typical of numerous other authors. This is how Tibi begins his piece on Iranian foreign affairs:

> Shiite Muslims often practise their faith as an underground religion because they have a history of being persecuted by the Sunnis. For their own protection they developed the practice of *taqiyah* or the concealment of one's faith; thus their religious affiliation is not always immediately recognisable.

Somewhat later, Tibi mentions a visit by the Iranian President and Defence Minister to China where they also had talks on 'nuclear cooperation between the two countries'. He writes: 'Answering suspicions that Iran was working on a nuclear programme for military purposes, government spokesmen gave assurances that the Iranian-Chinese cooperation in this field was only for peaceful purposes. Is this *taqiyah*, the concealment of foreign policy?'

But an expert does not leave such a question hanging, and it was answered by the subheading: 'In the Middle East and Central Asia, Iran is guided by the practice of "Taqiyah".' And this is indeed Tibi's argument. Iran, he says, has reverted 'to the politics of hegemony in the Gulf, which it had followed under the deposed Shah' – an undoubtedly accurate observation. But this was being done secretly, entirely in accordance with Shiite tradition. He then goes on to discuss the rivalry between Iran and Turkey, which is also active in Central Asia. Tibi continues:

> In contrast to the Khomeini era with its loud market crier's rhetoric, which was untypical for the Shiites, Iranian politicians today conduct their affairs quietly; thereby reverting to the Shiite tradition of *taqiyah* ... They act without speaking of their political aims, entirely in the spirit of 'concealment'; that is, they conceal their aims – even in their politics of hegemony – to the point of denial of their real identity.

You may well rub your eyes at this point. The argument – if it is one – has become clear: Iran conducts a special form of foreign affairs; and this is to be explained by its *religious history*, by the Shiite tradition. This is elegant and very convenient; an analysis of Iran's and its neighbours' *interests* is now superfluous.

Iran then is following a policy of hegemony and is doing so discreetly and secretly. This much is true. But what would be the alternative? To announce openly that it wants to bring the Gulf under its control? To place its atomic programme on display and grant CNN the filming rights? Almost all powers with hegemonic ambitions carry out their policies discreetly, they conceal and deny their intentions, and if necessary they lie through their teeth. During and after the Second World War, the USA and the Soviet Union conducted their atomic programmes in great secrecy. Israel has yet to admit its possession of atomic weapons. Pakistan denies having a military atomic programme. The Soviet intervention in Afghanistan was in order to 'secure world peace', just as the occupation of Czechoslovakia in 1968 was naturally an answer to 'a brother's cry for help'. The conquest of Grenada in the Caribbean by the USA in October 1983 was to help 'free hostages' (although there were no hostages), and to avert a threat to national security. Why is it necessary, and how is it meaningful, to bestow quasi-religious consecration on such a banal matter: that states conceal or gloss over their politics of power. When just about all states behave in the same way, why, in Iran's case, is it attributable to religious history?

There is a point to this senseless argument. Bassam Tibi constantly confirms the religious bias of the Arabs or the ways of thinking of other Muslims (in this article in the shape of 'verbose' Arabs) and their lack of secularism, while he presents himself as enlightened and secular. But here (and not only here) he for no reason ascribes a religious source to Iranian politics, where rational and secular considerations would have offered an entirely sufficient explanation. This of course makes it possible to go on to philosophise about the religious nature of Middle Eastern politics.

The logic of this instructive article is further clarified by the conclusion. 'Iran no longer speaks of the "export of the Islamic revolution"' – correct. Yet the accusation is now one of 'concealment'. In other words: if the Iranian dictatorship proclaims a policy of exporting its revolution (which could potentially include the totally secular aspect of offensive power politics), it is reproached for this. As soon as Iran no longer speaks of it, then – things can only get worse – it is concealing its policies. Tibi has successfully demonstrated how it is possible to immunise oneself against rational critique. Analysis becomes superfluous. Since we know that the Iranian government is Shiite, it naturally conducts a 'Shiite foreign policy'. It is thus possible to replace political analysis with religious and religious-historical deductions, all in the name of Western secular rationality.

To underline the main point once again: my criticism of a typically Western sham argument in no way constitutes sympathy for the Iranian dictatorship and its politics of hegemony. Yet even a brutal dictatorship should be analysed using the methods of Aristotelian logic. Even a dictatorship based on religion, such as Iran's, can do things for purely pragmatic or power political reasons (and this is not uncommon). Baghdad and Tehran both want to control the Gulf region and so does the USA. All three have enough solid economic, political and strategic reasons without needing a religious one. Nonetheless, none of these states would openly admit to this. Significantly, not only the Tehran mullahs, but Saddam Hussein and George Bush have all formulated their battle for supremacy in the Gulf in religious terms: jihad versus crusade.

The concept of the 'Islamic threat' thrives on imputing religious motives to the actions of Middle Eastern politicians in order then to complain about their strong religious orientation. This method is often a way of avoiding having to examine the problems and arguments of the Other. Let us take the example of one of the most complicated of all phenomena, Middle Eastern terrorism. It would be completely absurd to believe that this terrorism had arisen from ideological or even religious sources, as the expert on terrorism Tophoven would have us believe. It is far more plausible that it arose because sections of society and civil movements (in Lebanon, for example) saw no other possible way of exerting political influence. Without the Israeli invasion of Lebanon and the long occupation of South Lebanon, without Israel's undisputed military and political dominance there, it would not have been possible for Shiite terrorism to emerge in the form it did. This fact does not justify terrorist crimes, but helps us to understand connections. Without the West's support of Israeli policy and without the Western intervention in Lebanon in 1982–4 (with American, French, British and Italian troops) so many Western citizens would hardly have become victims of kidnapping and hostage taking. The Lebanese Shiites had nothing else with which they could, politically and in a narrower sense militarily, seriously oppose the occupying Israelis, the Western troops or the power structure of their own country. They would not have had a ghost of a chance in 'open battle'. Using guerrilla tactics, raids, kidnappings and assassination attempts they were able to deal very painful blows to their enemies despite their own weakness. In fact using these methods they were even able to drive the American and West European troops from their country in a relatively short space of time. The attacks on the American, French and Israeli headquarters in Lebanon resulted in hundreds dead and buildings completely destroyed – military attacks which would not have been possible using conventional means.

Essentially, such strategies have nothing to do with 'fanaticism', 'irrationality' or other similar psychological categories. They have plainly something to do with violent, unscrupulous, but ultimately extremely 'rational' behaviour (entirely in the Western sense): to achieve the maximum effect using the limited means at one's disposal. This is precisely what was achieved: the Western powers abandoned Lebanon in a virtual panic, and Israel too had to withdraw. What other tactics would have had such a result?

Clearly, there is no need to take cover under religious considerations in order to analyse Shiite terrorism.[44] One should only resort to supernatural or psychological explanations when it is no longer possible to get anywhere using other means of political analysis.

It goes without saying that the arguments put forward here do not mean that the religiosity of political participants must be peripheral for them (subjectively speaking). The opposite is true. Of course Shiite terrorists can be very religious people and derive strength for their deeds from their faith. But for most political questions this is of secondary importance – just as it is inconsequential whether or not George Bush really believed in the 'crusade-like' nature of the Gulf War or the godly reasons for the collapse of Soviet communism. Or, to return to an earlier example, even if the Iranian regime does place its foreign policy in a religious context and regards it as 'Islamic foreign policy', it still does not mean that the secretive nature of its ambitions for supremacy must therefore have a religious basis.

## Western Foreign Policy

The 'Islamic threat' in Western foreign policy was the subject of our consideration. The conclusions are apparently paradoxical. On the one hand, we have found examples where the perception of Islam as 'the enemy' (as examined by Andrea Lueg, Chapter 1) has made its way into foreign policy. This is not only true of reporting on foreign affairs in the media, but also of certain aspects such as terrorism and foreign policies regarding Iran or the Algerian Islamic party, the FIS. Even in the field of foreign affairs, it is assumed or at least believed that the actions of countries shaped by Islam or of some of their people or movements are primarily motivated by religion – something we would consider unrealistic in our own cultural area.

It is nonetheless clear that the core of Western foreign policy is not particularly affected by the notion of the Islamic threat, but only categorises Islam or its Islamist variants according to the varying contexts. It is clear that the West's Middle Eastern policies are primarily determined by the analysis of economic and power interests, not by the evaluation of a religion. The West only fears the Islamic threat in a religious context, when certain concrete interests are threatened. Within this setting the West sees both good and bad Muslims, good and bad fundamentalists. Pro-American or pro-Western Islamist forces can be as intolerant, fanatical or missionary as their anti-Western colleagues – we are reminded of Saudi Arabia or the Afghan Mujahidin. In such cases it is not a question of an 'Islamic threat' but simply of 'local colour'.

The idea of the Islamic threat has only limited use in foreign affairs. On the one had it is extremely attractive, as it can step in as the natural replacement for the lost 'enemy' of the Soviet Union/communism. The justification of a heavily armed military apparatus and a foreign policy aimed at establishing supremacy in the Gulf needs a plausible basis, a credible enemy. And this 'enemy' must be more than just an enemy, it must encompass an extensive ideology, as did Marxism-Leninism. 'Islam' or 'Islamic fundamentalism' offer themselves as ideal examples.

On the other hand, this creates problems. Many of the West's allies are themselves regimes which belong to the Islamic cultural area, some of them even fundamentalist. It would therefore be difficult to keep up an anti-Islamic, or even an only anti-Islamist, crusade. It would either encounter considerable problems of credibility, or would put off and lose the West important allies. For this reason, there is a kind of unstable in-between state where the perceived 'Islamic threat' in foreign policy is concerned. The threat is frequently conjured up in colourful, almost lyrical terms, depending on the economic conditions in various regions or countries. And suddenly there is silence, no more is said about Islamist threats. When the fight against Saddam Hussein was in the forefront Iran was no longer a popular threat, but a factor to be included diplomatically in the anti-Iraq front or at least regarded as neutral. Somewhat later, there is again increasingly talk of the Iranian threat, which is in fact worse than the Iraqi one: now the Islamic threat is re-emerging.[45] This pendulum, swinging in accordance with the prevailing political situation and opportunities, will also determine the West's relations with and policies towards Islamic and Islamist regimes in the future.

What is remarkable is the divergence between the woodcut images of 'the enemy' for internal consumption in the media, and the paradoxical use of this image of Islam in foreign affairs. While the tabloid press and other media are often virtually hysterical, disseminating grossly exaggerated horror scenarios and engaging in emotionally overladen sham reporting, foreign policy is guided at least partially by relatively sober evaluations determined more by self-interest and less by fears. Western policies towards the Middle East may be false in this sense, and may even single-mindedly pursue Western self-interest, at times brutally, with little regard for the lives of people there. But on the whole they are coldly and calculatedly rational. Only in exceptional cases are they given to creating bogey men, which are usually concocted for home consumption.

How are we to understand this disparity?

Two main reasons come to mind. First, foreign affairs remain the preserve of an elite. Home affairs, economic and social policies have a wide lobby, where pressure groups force discussion and make demands. Foreign affairs by contrast are of interest to a minority, a relatively small elite, and they are only occasionally bothered by grassroots movements on individual problems – the 'deployment of new arms' and the peace movement are important examples of this exception to the rule. Emotionalising and sensational 'enemy' image-building are, however, intended for wider mass consumption, and have little attraction for the ruling elite. The guardians of Western oil interests could hardly consider popular writing on the unmasking of the 'Islamic threat' to be relevant.

A second reason for the dichotomy between the domestic and foreign policy perceptions of Islam is that the general notion of a threat from the Middle East and Islam is only a pretext, not a real concern. The perception of the Islamic threat has virtually nothing to do with the Middle East or Islam, but everything to do with the establishment of an inter-Western identity. It is about reassuring ourselves, about reassuring each other of how rational, enlightened and sensible we Westerners are. The need for this has of course arisen from the regrettable fact that standards of civilisation in Europe are not high, and are constantly being dragged down by explosive set-backs. Fascism, Stalinism and other archaic phenomena such as the wars in the Balkans, the civil war in Northern Ireland, or racism in the USA which exceeds even what is prevalent in Europe – to mention but a few notable examples – should urge us to be careful in our estimation of Western civilisation. The burning of Lebanese girls in the Lower Rhine region and other similar manifestations of the 'soul of the people' are hardly indicative of deeply anchored civilising values in the Christian West. By caricaturing different cultures, by arbitrarily and wilfully misrepresenting Islamic societies, we grant ourselves absolution. *Others* are fanatical, we are not. *Others* are irrational, we are not.

It is by and large evident that the view of Islam as a threat is deeply anchored in the minds of European public opinion. A diffuse and often irrational fear of Islam, of 'the Arabs', of a different culture and of the poverty of the Third World, all this and more combines with racism and xenophobia to make a depressing, dark and murky mixture. In domestic affairs all these fears exist, and the perception of threat is fully developed. But in the field of foreign affairs it is latent. It is accessible, just below the surface, and is not always activated and exploited for foreign policy purposes. There is both a reassuring and alarming aspect to this situation. What is reassuring is the conclusion that Western foreign policy vis-à–vis the Middle East is characterised by an interest in political and economic domination, and by a readiness to occasionally sacrifice some hundred thousand lives (Arab of course) in the pursuance of Western interests. The West then is not conducting a 'crusade' or a policy guided by its racist perception of 'the enemy', but 'merely' an imperialist policy. If that's the good news, what's the bad news?

What is really threatening is that this imperialist policy can fall back on the latent emotionalising mentioned above. If Western strategists should decide on further interventions, wars or other new forms of neo-colonialist domination, in order to achieve their interests – then the politico-psychological prerequisites needed to justify any political or military adventure at home are easily available. The latent perceived threat can be activated at any time. Whenever necessary, the 'Islamic threat' against which we must 'defend' ourselves can be used.

This is exactly what the prominent American political scientist and Pentagon consultant Samuel Huntington tried to do in 1993 with his essay 'The Clash of Civilizations' which appeared in the journal *Foreign Affairs*. What had previously remained in the background of the foreign policy debate in the West, as a *potential* danger (in contrast to the flustered reactions of much of the media), was now brought on to centre stage by Huntington. In the process the conceptual theories of a representative of the foreign affairs establishment now entirely corresponded with the stereotypes and perceptions characteristic of the media and popular literature.

It is my hypothesis that the fundamental source of conflict in this new world will not be primarily ideological or primarily economic.

The great divisions among humankind and the dominating source of conflict will be cultural. Nation states will remain the most powerful actors in world affairs, but the principal conflicts of global politics will occur between nations and groups of different civilizations. The clash of civilizations will be the battle lines of the future.[46]

Huntington is not talking about abstract conflicts between unnamed civilisations, but about specific international conflicts. He has discovered a 'Confucian-Islamic connection that has emerged to challenge Western interests, values, and power' and believes 'a central focus of conflict for the immediate future will be between the West and several Islamic-Confucian states.'[47]

Within this anti-Western front, he apparently considers the Islamic civilisations to be the more dangerous. The burden of history is partly responsible for this. 'Conflict along the fault line between Western and Islamic civilizations has been going on for 1300 years.' In this connection he talks about the 'warfare between Arabs and the West', that culminated in the 1990–1 Gulf War.[48]

He refers to the current conflicts in Europe and Asia when he mentions the

crescent-shaped Islamic bloc of nations from the bulge of Africa to Central Asia ... Violence also occurs between Muslims, on the one hand, and Orthodox Serbs in the Balkans, Jews in Israel, Hindus in India, Buddhists in Burma and Catholics in the Philippines. Islam has bloody borders'.[49]

Huntington sees this form of conflict occurring in the wake of the Cold War as determining the structure of the international system, even though the Islamic front's position against the West, as he perceives it, is only a part of a wider problem. It is in fact a battle of 'The West against the rest'.

Huntington's image of Islam (or of other Asian cultures) is hardly original. It follows the current stereotypes and clichés of popular literature and some of the media. Yet he manages brilliantly to embellish these reheated fears pseudo-scientifically and elevate them ideologically. His success is in making the old clichés acceptable in the foreign policy debate. For Huntington, Islam is ideologically hostile and anti-Western. It is also a military threat in itself due to Chinese ('Confucian') arms supplies. Islam is bloody, with a long warring tradition against the West. (The fact that Muslims have often been the victims rather than the perpetrators of violence from Bosnia to India hardly troubles him.)

He is not, then, concerned with an analysis of the interests or the political forces of the Middle East. This is largely superfluous, since in any case there is an unbridgeable gap and fundamental enmity between the two cultures. His policy suggestions are derived from this view:

> To limit the expansion of the military strength of Confucian and Islamic states; to moderate the reduction of Western military capabilities and maintain military superiority in East and South West Asia; to exploit differences and conflicts among Confucian and Islamic states; to support in other civilizations groups sympathetic to Western values and interests.

Once this point had been reached, the West would have to maintain 'the economic and military power necessary to protect its interests in relation to these civilizations'.[50]

Huntington's entire argument about Islam and civilisations is full of contradictions and superficialities. But this is of little consequence, since it is only meant as a politically motivated sales pitch to secure Western superiority in all areas. That is why Islam must be dangerous and irreconcilable, and that is why the West cannot afford to disarm itself excessively in the wake of the Cold War. It must arm itself against the threat. This is the essence of Huntington's thesis, and everything else, including the laws of Aristotelian logic, are consistently subordinated to it. What is significant, however, is that the rationale of his perceived threat is not based on an analysis of the interests or policies of countries or political powers in the Middle East, but on his contradictory formulation of 'civilising' basic categories. According to Huntington, it is not the clash of interests that leads to conflict; the simple fact is that differences between cultures engender war. In a certain sense you could call his argument 'culturally racist'. The Muslims (or the Chinese) are *different* from us and *therefore* dangerous. Unlike in classic racism, this difference is not genetically but culturally based. There is such a gulf between their values and ways of thinking and ours that understanding or cross-pollination is almost unthinkable. Only military solutions can promise results.

Herein lies the originality of Huntingtonian theories: the earlier division between the hysterical perception of threat in elements of the media and the cool debate of the foreign affairs establishment based on realpolitik is removed, and the clichés and stereotypes and erstwhile concept of 'enemy' are to be made the point of departure for Western foreign policy. And all this in defence of Western rationality and other values of the Enlightenment. This can only mean two things for Western foreign policy. It can either use these theories to justify its policies, without actually accepting their content; foreign policy makers would thus continue to be guided by calculatedly rational imperialist interests, while analysing the interests of the other protagonists (such as in the Middle East), and use the alleged clash of civilisations for domestic consumption alone, in order to win support at home for these policies. Such practice would be cynical, but the preferable alternative. Or, and this would be dangerous, the political elite could take Huntington's theories seriously and make them the guiding principle of their actions. This would result in a massive reideologisation of foreign policy, which would be directed less by realities or real interests, and more by fantasies of our own making. We would then be acting in exactly the way for which we reproach Islamic fundamentalists. This might result in the countries of Europe and North America actually following a policy of 'the West against the rest'. This would itself be interpreted all over the Third World as a 'Western conspiracy' to rule the world. This would surely result in a drastic escalation of conflicts along the lines of black versus white, Christian versus Islamic, the West against the Third World. A self-fulfilling prophecy does not have to be original or sensible to have disastrous consequences. If we extol a culturally defined racism as the leitmotif of our foreign policy we should not be surprised when other cultures consequently encourage isolationist tendencies and anti-Western confrontation.

## Notes

1   'Der Duft des Imam', *Der Spiegel*, February 1992, p. 108. The passages quoted here from *Der Spiegel* are only of an exemplary nature. For our purposes it is not worth quoting from several other articles from the magazine as the picture would not change. A new article, which could have been cited equally well is 'Unser Marsch hat begonnen – Der islamische Fundamentalismus: Eine Revolte gegen den Westen und seine Weltordnung', *Der Spiegel*, May 1993, p. 108–20. Perhaps we should also mention that *Der Spiegel* cultivates a particular style for this theme: sober and realistic passages and wildly emotionalising sections are blatantly juxtaposed. The result is naturally that the rabble-rousing passages not only contradict the more considered ones but also conceal and undermine them.

All the italics in this and in subsequent quotes are the author's.

2 'Der Duft des Imam', *Der Spiegel*, February 1992, p. 108.

3 J. Miller, 'The Challenge of Radical Islam', *Foreign Affairs*, Vol. 72, No. 2, Spring 1993, p. 45.

4 'The Dark Side of Islam', *Time Magazine*, 4 October 1993, p. 62.

5 *US News and World Report*, 22 March 1993.

6 Y. Bodansky, *Target America – Terrorism in the U.S. Today*, New York: SPI Books, 1992, p. 1.

7 John L. Esposito, *The Islamic Threat – Myth or Reality?*, New York and Oxford: Oxford University Press, 1992, p. 175.

8 H. Bräker, *Es wird kein Friede sein – der islamische Orient im Zangengriff von West und Ost*, Munich: Artemis & Winker Publ., 1992, p. 232.

9 Secretary Baker, 'America's Stake in the Persian Gulf', Prepared statement before the House Foreign Affairs Committee, Washington DC, 4 September 1990, *US Department of State Dispatch, Bureau of Public Affairs*, Vol. 1, No. 2, 10 September 1990, p. 69.

10 James Clapper, 'Regional Flashpoints for Military Conflict' – Excerpts: Clapper congressional testimony, USIS Public Diplomacy Query Index and Text Database on CD-Rom, Text Link 210716, 22 January 1992.

11 Former US Defense Secretary Cheney, 'Cheney Says Ignoring Iraq would be Dire Error' – Excerpts: Cheney statement to committee in USIS Public Diplomacy Query Index and Text Database on CD-Rom, Text Link 154318, 11 September 1990.

12 Secretary Baker, 'America's Stake in the Persian Gulf', p. 69.

13 S. T. Hunter, 'Persian Gulf Security: Lessons of the Past and the Need for New Thinking', *SAIS Review*, Vol. 12, No. 1, Winter/Spring 1992, p. 156–7.

14 The author has written on the structure of Western interests elsewhere. As this essay is only concerned with this theme in passing, we will not go into this point in any depth here. See, however, among others: J. Hippler, *Pax Americana? – Hegemony or Decline*, London: Pluto Press, 1994, pp. 113–18; and 'Krieg am Golf – Modellkrieg für die Dritte Welt?', in V. Matthies and J. Betz (eds), *Jahrbuch Dritte Welt 1992*, Munich: Beck Publ., 1991, pp. 86–101, here pp. 88–93.

15 Hunter, 'Persian Gulf Security', p. 157.

16 E. W. Anderson and K. H. Rashidian, *Iraq and the Continuing Middle East Crisis*, New York 1991, p. 76ff.

17 On the history of Hamas, see, among others, 'Hamas makes it to the centrestage', *The Middle East*, February 1993, p. 9ff.

18 'Building an Enemy – America, Israel and Arab States Created the Islamic Militants They Now Fear', *Newsweek*, 15 February 1993, pp. 10–12, here p. 11.

19 *Time Magazine*, 4 October 1993, p. 60.

20 Reagan 'Deeply Saddened' by Zia's Death, USIS Public Diplomacy Query Index and Text Database on CD-Rom, Text Link 39954, 17 August 1988.

21 'Building an Enemy' – America, *Newsweek*, pp. 10–12, here pp. 10–11.

22 J. Miller, 'The Islamic Wave', *The New York Times Magazine*, 31 May 1992, pp. 25, 42.

23 J. Liminski, 'Aus dem Schatten der Moschee: Europas Bedrohung durch den islamischen Radikalismus', *Das Parlament*, No. 3/4, 10/17 January 1992.

24 ibid.

25 International Terrorism, Insurgency, and Drug Trafficking: Present Trends in Terrorist Activity, Joint Hearings Before the Committee on Foreign Relations and the Committee on the Judiciary, United States Senate, 15 May 1985, Committee Print, p. 239.

26 R. Tophoven, *Sterben für Allah – die Schiiten und der Terrorismus*, Herford: Busse Seewald Publ., 1991, p. 49.

27 ibid., p. 174.

28 The proclamation of a holy war by some statesmen or politicians can be irrelevant. The declaration of holy war can be approximated to former US President George Bush calling for a 'crusade' in the Gulf. Both are cases of metaphors that sound good and have nothing to do with holy wars or crusades.

29 It is worth pointing out here that Tophoven also summarises and misjudges fundamentalism. 'Fundamentalism' often aims at its own version of 'modernisation', and is not uncommonly aimed at the fact that the West does not allow Islamic countries such a modernisation, and makes it impossible using economic means and political and military superiority. In this book Azmy Bishara rightly argues that fundamentalism is itself a 'modern' social current and cannot be understood as simply an anti-modernity counter-movement.

30 Tophoven, *Sterben für Allah*, p. 200ff.

31 ibid., p. 181.

32 I recall a conversation with a well–placed interlocutor from the US government, on my return from a trip to Libya. He was mainly interested in knowing if I thought Gaddafi was mentally ill.

33  Liminski, 'Aus dem Schatten'.
34  Miller, 'The Islamic Wave', p. 38.
35  Personal communication with an Iraqi diplomat, transcribed from a tape recording.
36  Paul D. Wolfowitz, U.S. National Security Strategy for the 1990s, in USIS Public Diplomacy Query Index and Text Database on CD Rom, Text Link 120876, 8 December 1989.
37  Bush Cautions U.S. Must Maintain Strong Defense, Speech to Commonwealth Club of San Francisco, in USIS Public Diplomacy Query, Index and Text Database on CD Rom, Text Link 127739, 7 February 1990.
38  Hunter, 'Persian Gulf Security', p. 161.
39  Bush Outlines New World Order, Economic Plans, State of the Union Message, in USIS Public Diplomacy Query Index and Text Database on CD Rom, Text Link 212310, 28 January 1992.
40  *US News and World Report*, quoted from *Der Spiegel*, January 1991, p. 107.
41  Quote taken from S. P. Tillman, *The United States in the Middle East – Interests and Obstacles*, Bloomington: Indiana University Press, 1982, pp. 45–6.
42  Quoted from ibid., p. 46.
43  *Frankfurter Allgemeine Zeitung*, 14 October 1992, p. 14.
44  A note on terminology is appropriate here. Not everything that has been described as 'terrorism' in the West can really go under this label. When they have a political background, the kidnapping of civilians, bomb attacks on shopping streets and school buses are undisputedly terrorist acts . By contrast, violent attacks on purely military targets are often of a 'military' rather than terrorist nature, even though they may be carried out using unconventional weapons and/or methods.
45  An example is the article 'Iran – The Threat that Gets Overlooked', *Newsweek*, 25 January 1993, p. 25.
46  S. P. Huntington, 'The Clash of Civilizations?', *Foreign Affairs*, Vol. 72, No. 3, Summer 1993, p. 22.
47  ibid., pp. 45–8.
48  ibid., p. 31.
49  ibid., pp. 34–5.
50  ibid., p. 49.

# 7

# Conclusion: Dealing with Islam

*Jochen Hippler and Andrea Lueg*

In this book, we have argued that the Western media, journalists and politicians tend towards an irrational way of dealing with Islam or Islamism. We have emphasised that the perceived 'Islamic threat' has little to do with the realities of the Middle East and more to do with the West's need to reassure itself, while reality is used very selectively or as a background setting. We have also warned against stirring up emotions and inciting hysteria about Islam. The contributors to this book have not tried to reveal the 'true Islam'. After all, the true Islam is as non-existent as the true Christianity. Or to be more precise: what does or does not constitute the 'correct' interpretation of Islam or Christianity is not a question of political analysis, but one of belief. Besides, we think that this question should be settled between the believers and by themselves. This is not our concern. For this reason, in three of the six chapters in this book, Islam is only a secondary subject. We are far more concerned with considering our own Western way of thinking, and we hope to have made some contribution in this direction.

It would, however, be unsatisfying to end this book without at least having given some basic suggestions as to how non-Islamic, or indeed non-Christian, Europeans might come to terms with Islam and especially Islamism. We have not after all pleaded 'for Islam' in this book, but only that it be treated no differently from Christianity or Judaism. Since we (the editors) do not believe in God ourselves, in either his Christian, Muslim or any other manifestation, it could not have been our aim to publish a 'pro-Islamic' book. We were far more concerned with rationally discussing religious phenomena. For many, elements of the current hostile view of Islam bear pre- or anti-Enlightenment traits, however critical of religion they may be presented as being. Islam is often dealt with by authors who at first argue like Islamic mullahs – that the 'true' Islam is ostensibly basically fundamentalist, its modern forms only diluted deviations – in order then to discover its backwardness. This sort of intellectual dishonesty offends us, even though we are neither Muslims nor Christians.

How then do we propose to come to terms with Islam or Islamist movements? On a general level, we consider a secular approach to be the only sensible one. Moreover, Islam should not be measured using different criteria from those we use for Christianity for example, and events in societies shaped by Islam must on the whole be measured with the same yardsticks. Finally, it would be helpful to curb our own cultural arrogance and not to overestimate the level of civilised and enlightened behaviour of societies in Europe and the USA.

By these very general observations, we mean the following. A secular approach would mean that even where Muslims are concerned, we do not immediately assume that everything must have a religious basis, and we interpret their real interests (which may be religiously coloured) and see their arguments in relation to these interests. Not every religious-sounding phrase necessarily has a religious meaning. Often such modes of expression are only a culturally determined way of speaking about economic, social or political matters. It does not seem to us that paying attention to the content rather than the form of expression is asking for too much. The reservations of a Muslim towards 'the West' may be based on a number of very real experiences that do not always have religious roots. The earlier experience of colonial oppression and exploitation, the experience of cultural arrogance, of the West's economic and technological supremacy, the exploitation of the natural resources of the Middle East, the experience of double standards or military domination – these and much else are reasons enough for scepticism or hostility towards the West. Whether someone then chooses to express this scepticism in secular or religious terms is their business. Criticism of the West or of one's own regime should not be automatically ignored simply because religious terms are used. References to European and American politics of supremacy or to the neo-imperialist policies of the West in the Middle East do not become invalid just because they are made by a practising Muslim or Christian.

A secular approach also means not judging all Muslims by their pious gestures. Religious hypocrisy, a display of religious practices or symbols, or pious self-deception are not limited to Europe, the USA or the Christian cultural area, but are as well loved in the Middle East as they are over here. Islam is exploited for political, economic and social purposes to the same extent. Who in Germany would suggest that the 'Christian Democratic Party' is a religious or quasi-religious organisation? From where do we get the naivety of not noticing similar exploitation of religion in a neighbouring cultural area? Whoever believes in taking every religious utterance from the Middle East at its word, should do us the favour of considering President Bill Clinton to be a Christian fundamentalist, since in his very first speech as President he beseeched God to guide him in his office.

Furthermore, there is a reflex tendency to refer all political conflicts in the Middle East back to some development of early Islam, preferably the life of Mohammed or the Koran. This relieves us of the necessity to think or analyse, because according to this view, not only today's conflicts but all future ones have already been analysed: that's what the Muslims are like, for it is written in the Koran, and that is what the Prophet said. Applying this method, Middle Eastern academics could be tempted to explain the wars in former Yugoslavia by reference to the Bible or the life of Jesus.

We have in fact already come to our next suggestion: that we use the same standards for the people of the Middle East that we use for ourselves. Of course this does not mean denying cultural differences or believing that table manners in both regions must necessarily be standardised. First, it must be accepted that Christianity and Islam are to be treated equally in principle. There are good reasons to argue that Christianity (at least in the form in which it has been handed down) or indeed all religion is basically irrational. 'Believing' is no rational act, even if many theologians and philosophers of just about all cultural groups would have it so. And belief in a God (or Gods) is in essence an extremely authoritarian matter: a God is above the people, is omnipotent and omniscient, and people are subordinate to him and should subordinate themselves to him, even when they do not understand his supposed wisdom. This is without doubt authoritarian and irrational, and in principle far removed from rational analysis. Such criticism can be applied equally to Islam and Christianity. Since their times of origin, both religions have worked against women (even though their respective founders and some devotees may not have necessarily so intended it). Both religions and their holy books portray a strangely archaic ideology hardly applicable to current times and social structures, and they can only be salvaged from these anachronistic constraints by bold and creative interpretation. Such criticisms should be discussed seriously: but to assume that Christianity, or societies shaped by Christianity, are somehow especially refined or enlightened, or that they are natural or quasi-natural, while the sister-religion is uncommonly medieval, is simply vain and idle nonsense. In some respects Christianity is 'more modern', in others Islam,[1] and again, the details should be discussed by the faithful. But fairness and intellectual honesty demand that two so closely related religions should not be treated differently.

Those who see Islam as 'the enemy', however, are in any case not interested in such questions. The authors of this image do not compare like with like: Christianity with Islam, or the realities of Europe with those of the Middle East. As a rule they are prone to comparing a *religion* (Islam) with a *region* (or *society*) ('the West'). And if you ask the wrong questions you do not get the right answers.

We have spoken of applying the same yardsticks, and there is something else we mean by this. Of course all the things that anti-Islam hysterics keep telling us about do exist in Islamic societies. There is fanaticism, dogmatism, large-scale oppression of women, reactionary narrow-mindedness, racism, and ideological and religious blindness. There is also the danger of the proliferation of weapons of mass destruction, massacres, terrorism and the abuse of human rights. It would be totally absurd to wish to ignore all this or to dispute it or play it down. But because we have not written a book about the Middle East, or about the 'Orient', but about our Western ways of thinking, such phenomena have only been treated perfunctorily. The reason for the theme of this book was not that we would overlook such phenomena or find them pleasant. We only seek to warn against the common practice of jumping to conclusions. Many of these terrible things have little to do with Islam but have other origins; and quite a few of these shocking phenomena also exist in 'modern' Western societies. Fanaticism, for example, can have secular roots, even when its bearers might deny this. This is in no way justifies it, but reminds us of the need to apply the common standards that we have spoken of above.

Before we get het up about the fanaticism of others, we should not deny the fanaticism of our own culture. When German youths want to burn down refugee hostels, this also has something to do with fanaticism and irrationality, not just with alcohol and a lack of perspective. Yet few of us would think of suggesting these crimes had religious roots, or that they spring from the Christian traditions of the West. Thus, the fanaticism and irrationality of people in the Middle East are not always connected to religion. Often it is a case of general human limitation, which arises from the given living conditions. Petty-bourgeois conformism, dogmatism, knowing-it-all, racist arrogance, all exist in the Middle East as they do here. And equally, we should examine the real reasons for them by looking at the real situations, not by thinking we already know: it must have to do with the religion, with Islam. This view is not only superficial and arrogant, but also amounts to a mystification of social correlations. If the same or similar phenomena exist in both cultural areas, then we should be looking for common origins of these phenomena, and should not automatically make one of the two religions responsible for them. Where there are examples of hostility to women in Islamic societies, then we must analyse their causes with the same care that we apply to social research in the West. Hostility and discrimination against women can exist without there being religious reasons for it; and such a secular form of discrimination can be cloaked in religion to make it appear more legitimate.

Of course this does not mean that ideological and religious factors could not and would not play a role. Of course they do, just as secular misogyny in Europe has been influenced and stimulated by similar religious positions. Since religious traditions in the East have had a stronger influence on culture than they have had over here, they are naturally an important factor there. But once again: we must in the end analyse the influence of religious traditions on secular thinking and determine their relation to each other, instead of taking the easy way out by ignoring all other factors apart from religion.

The American journalist Christopher Dickey recently speculated on whether Islam really posed a threat.

> Hamas spokesman Abdel Aziz al-Rantisi, when asked repeatedly about the *positive* aspects of his faith, answers repeatedly: 'No stealing, no illegal sex, no liquor, no usury, no using women as a commodity to be bought and sold.' There is order. But in the end, this kind of fundamentalism is profoundly secular. In this mode Islam can be exploited to perpetuate the rule of a single family, as in Saudi Arabia, or serve as a vehicle for national ambitions like Iran's. Authoritarianism, expansionism, terrorism: these are real dangers, but familiar ones. Described as such, they can be dealt with dispassionately. Add the word Islam however, and suddenly there is a Western perception of menace out of all proportion to rational threats ...
>
> Should the West fear Islam? Not as such. But it is worth keeping a very close eye on those who carry its banner.

## Note

1    For example in the consistency of its monotheism.

# Notes on Contributors

**Professor Azmy Bishara** (b. 1956) lives in Jerusalem and teaches philosophy at the Bir Zeit University in the Occupied Territories. He is also doing research at the Van Leer Institute in Jerusalem, and specialises in the state and religion, politics and mythology, Marxism and Eurocentrism. He has published widely on Zionism, the Palestinian question, and conflict in the Middle East.

**Fred Halliday** (b.1946) is currently Professor of International Relations at the London School of Economics. He has published books on Iran, Yemen and the Cold War.

**Dr Jochen Hippler** (b. 1955) is a political scientist and Director of the Transnational Institute (TNI) in Amsterdam. He specialises in regional conflicts in the Third World; superpower policies of intervention; US foreign policy; the Near and Middle East and the development of a new world order following the end of the Cold War. He is the author of a number of books and essays. He lives in Cologne and Amsterdam.

**Professor Petra Kappert** (b. 1945) is a scholar of Islamic studies and teaches Turkish studies in the department of Near East Studies at the University of Hamburg. She specialises in research on the history and culture of the Ottoman empire, the Turkish Republic and the Turkic peoples of Central Asia as well as on Islam in Germany.

**Andrea Lueg** (b. 1962) is a freelance journalist based in Cologne. Her main interests are in the developing world, especially in the Middle Eastern countries, and in women in Islamic societies. She has made several research trips to the Middle East.

**Professor Reinhard Schulze** (b. 1953) teaches Islamic and Arabic studies at Bamberg University. Prior to this he was Professor of Oriental Philology at Bochum University. He specialises in research on the modern history of the Islamic world (from the sixteenth to the twentieth centuries), the sociology of Islamic culture and religion, and the history of Arabic literature from the sixteenth to the twentieth century.

# Index

Abbasid dynasty (Baghdad) 96
Abd al-Raziq, Sheikh Ali 92
Abduh, Muhammad 104
al-Afghani, Jamal al-Din 103–4
Afghanistan 121, 128–9
aggression, as characteristic of
   Islam 9
Ahmad ibn Hanbal 97
Alawiyya, religious sect 74
Algeria 108, 120, 121
   Muslim emigrants to France
   74
   nuclear programme 136
Ali ibn abu Talib, Caliph 91
apostasy 77–8
Arab Christians, and Arab nationalism 100
Arab nationalism 98–107
   hostility to West 126
   and Islam 99, 100, 102, 128
   and Israel 110
   secularisation of 101
Asim Efendi, Ottoman chronicler
   45
al-Asmawi, Muhammad Said 92
Atatuürk, Kemal 73, 95, 99
Austria–Hungary, Ottoman
   embassy in 43
authenticity (*asalah*), and
   rejection of modernity 58–9

Baghdad railway project 52–3
Baker, James (US Secretary of
   State) 120, 121, 125
al-Banna, Hassan, founder of
   Muslim Brotherhood 85, 91,
   105–6

Barreau, Jean-Claude
   on aggression in Islam 9, 13
   on superiority of West 21
Bible, Arabic translations of 36
*Bild Zeitung* (German newspaper)
   16
blasphemy 77–8, 80–1n
Bodansky, Yossef 118
Bonaparte, Napoleon *see*
   Napoleon Bonaparte
Bosnia 3, 11
Bräker, Hans 119
Bronner, Ethan 16
Bush, George (US President) 138,
   139
   on Zia 129

caliphate
   abolished (1924) 73, 95, 97
   history of 92, 95–7
Camp David Agreement (1978)
   140
Carter, Jimmy (US President) 140
CENTO pact (1955) 127
Cheney, R (US Defense Secretary)
   124–5
China
   cooperation with Iran 141
   as threat to West 148–9
Christianity
   Arab Christians 100
   origins of fundamentalism 12
   and Western politics 155–6
CIA (Central Intelligence
   Agency), in Afghanistan 128
Clapper, Lt Gen James (US
   Defense Intelligence) 123–4

Clinton, Bill (US President) 139,
    155–6
Cold War 126–7
    effect of end of 4
colonialism
    and Arab nationalism 100–1
    effect on Islamic identity 64
    in India 91
Commonwealth of Independent
    States (former USSR) 72,
    121
    *see also* Soviet Union
communism
    Islam as buffer against 126–31
    Islamic links with 74
Confucian culture, perceived
    connection with Islam
    148–9
Congress movement 64
Copts (Egypt) 108
crusade, use of term 139, 143,
    152n
Crusades, the 4

*Das Parlament* (German
    magazine) 2, 131
democracy
    in Middle East 12, 62, 123
    parliamentarianism 46
Denon, Dominique Virant,
    French chronicler 37
*Der Spiegel* (German magazine) 9,
    12, 150n
    on Islamic threat 117–18
    view of Islamic women 18
despotism, in Orient 34
Dickey, Christopher 158
diplomacy 42–4, 46
drugs, war on 4

economic problems
    in Middle East 14, 121–2
    and rise of nationalism 107
*Economist* (British magazine) 12
education, and modernisation in
    Ottoman empire 47, 49–50,
    51

Egypt
    application of Sharia 94
    and Arab nationalism 104
    and French Revolution 32
    growing instability 120
    independence from Ottoman
        empire (1811) 48
    modernisation in 47–8, 49–51
    Muslim Brotherhood 64, 85,
        90, 91, 92, 104–6
    Napoleon's invasion of (1798)
        21, 37–8, 57
    nationalist movements 87, 88,
        100–3, 108–9
    political religion in 89
    Wafd opposition party 104, 105
*EMMA* (German feminist
    magazine) 18
enemy
    must be different 20–1, 133,
        149–50
    Western need for concept of 2,
        4–5, 24–5, 131–2, 145
Enlightenment, the
    revised view of Orient 34
    and separation of state and
        religion 21
Esposito, John, *The Islamic Threat*
    118–19
ethnic territorial conflict 121
Europe
    boundaries with Islam 71, 148
    Islamic immigrants 72

fanaticism
    in Islam 2, 8, 13, 157
    of 'masses' 15
    in Western countries 23–4, 157
Fatimid dynasty (Tunis and
    Egypt) 96
First World War 54
Flügel, G., orientalist 36
France
    communist party connections
        with Muslims 74
    Enlightenment view of Orient
        34

'headscarf affair' 10, 17
influence on Oriental modernisation 42, 48–9
invasion of Egypt (1798) 21, 37–8
Islamic immigrants in 72, 73, 74, 76, 116
Ottoman diplomatic relations with 43–5, 46
freedom, concept of 45–6, 47–8
French Revolution
effect on Ottoman empire 32, 42–7
and religion 82
Fuad, King, of Egypt 112n
fundamentalism 12, 84–5, 112n, 152n
as political religion 83, 84–9
in Western countries 12, 23–4
*see also* Islam fundamentalism

Gaddafi, Col Muammar 119, 130
Germany
attacks on immigrants 2, 4, 146
Baghdad railway project 52–3
Green movement 84
Islamic immigrants in 18, 72, 73, 116
media views of Islam 7
Ottoman embassy established 43
romanticised view of Orient 32, 33–6, 41, 53–4
and threat of Islamic terrorism 134
al-Ghanouchi, Rachid 111
al-Ghazali, theologian 94
Goethe, Johann Wolfgang von, fascination with Orient 34–6
Great Britain
and Iran 79
Islamic immigrants in 72, 73, 77
occupation of Egypt (1882) 49, 50, 51
origins of Muslim immigrants 74, 76

Ottoman embassy in 43
Yemeni community in 74, 75, 76
Greece
conflict with Ottoman empire 38–9
uprising (1821) 46
Grenada 142
Gulf War
consequences of 120
military superiority of West 10, 21
and US interests 124–5
Gülhane decree of reform (1839) 46–7

Hafiz, Persian poet (d.1389) 34–5
*hakimiya* (rule of God) 90–1
Hamas group 128
Hanafi, Hasan 61
Hawa, Sa'id 102
Heine, Heinrich
image of Orient as feminine 39–40
on Napoleon 38–9
Hekmatyar, Gulbuddin, fundamentalist leader 128–9
Hiro, Dilip 112n
Hizbollah 133
campaign in Lebanon 111, 117
holy wars *see* crusades; jihad
human rights 22–3
Hunter, Shireen 125–6
Huntington, Samuel, conflict with Islam as inevitable 10–11, 147–50
al-Husri, Sat'a 100

Ibn Taymiyya, philosopher 104
ideology
Islam as 60–1
and religion 83, 156
immigrants
assimilation of 76–7
Islamic women as 18
political demands of 77

second-generation 73, 76
in US 10, 26
*see also* migration
Imperial Training Institute for
    Translation (1821) 47
Iran 108, 120–1, 145
    American embassy siege 117
    as buffer against USSR 127
    cooperation with China 141
    foreign policy 141–3
    influence over emigrants 75
    and Islamic fundamentalism
        79–80
    revolution 107, 116, 127–8
    rivalry with Iraq 123–4
    Sharia adopted as legislation
        93–4
Iran-Iraq war 99
Iraq 120
    influence over emigrants 75
    military strength of 137
    nuclear capability 3, 124
    rivalry with Iran 123–4
    seen by US as threat 124–5,
        145
irrationality, imputed to Arabs
    16–17, 119
Islam
    as ideology 60–1
    intellectual criticism of 66–7,
        79–80
    as social system 112n
    *see also* Islam (religion); Islamic
        culture
Islam (political)
    in crisis 107–11
    nationalist aspirations of
        104–5, 106–7
    *see also* Arab nationalism;
        Islamic countries
Islam (religion) 11–12, 60
    absence of criticism of 66
    connection between state and
        religion 13–14, 22, 62–3,
        65–6, 83–4, 92–3, 95–7
    conversion to 72, 99
    fragmentation of 73–4, 75, 76

and Islamic nationalism 87,
    107
    threatened by secularism 77–9
    as unifying force 33, 72, 97
    Western fear of 25–7, 66,
        132–3
    Western images of 7, 156–8
    *see also* Islamic fundamental-
        ism; Koran
Islamic citizenry, concept of 65–7
Islamic Conference Organisation
    (1966) 102
Islamic countries
    criticism of West 28, 126,
        138–9
    debate on modernisation in
        23, 57–8, 59–61, 67n
    defined 5n
    and non-Arab Muslims 99
    rise of nationalism in 71–2, 87,
        102
    *see also* Middle East; national-
        ism; Orient
Islamic culture
    as alien 2, 10–11, 25–7, 119
    and collective identity 58,
        62–3, 75–6
    intellectual 58, 66–7 and n,
        69n
    and role of religion 61, 62–3
    as threat 10, 148–50
    threatened 14–15, 28, 77
    *see also* Islam (religion)
Islamic fundamentalism 6n,
    78–9, 103, 130
    anti-communism of 127–9
    rejection of modernity 12–13,
        23
    Western fear of 2–3, 12–13, 79,
        132, 139
    Western use of 130–1
Islamic Jihad
    Lebanon 117
    organisations 108
Islamic law *see* Sharia
Islamic politics
    history of 63–5

Koranic concepts in 91–2
*see also* Islam (political)
Islamic Salvation Front (FIS),
  Algeria 136, 144
Islamic World League 75
Ismail, Khedive of Egypt 51
Israel 108
  and Muslim Brotherhood 128
  nuclear weapons 136
  state of 98, 103
  and terrorism 143–4
  war with 99, 110
  and Western policies in Middle
    East 126
  *see also* Judaism

*jahiliya* (dark age), concept of
  90–1
Jama'at al-Islamiyah (Egypt) 90,
  94, 109
Jama'at al-Tabligh (Society of
  Propagation) 74, 75
Jama'at-i-Islam (Pakistan) 75
jihad
  concept of 9
  use of 109
Jordan 106, 108
Judaism 86, 89
  *see also* Israel; Zionism

Kashmir 121
al-Kawakibi, Abd al-Rahman 100,
  104
Kemal, Namik 51
Kharijite sect (7th century) 91–2
Khomeini, Ayatollah
  call for jihad 133
  on *The Satanic Verses* 77
Kirkpatrick, Jeane, US
  ambassador to UN 16
Koran 62, 156
  Islam as perfected religion 60
  on jihad 9
  political interpretation of
    91–5
  on women 19
Kurds 116, 120, 121

Lebanon 107, 116, 143–4
Lewis, Bernard 42, 92, 97
  and Arab nationalism 98
Libya 103, 116, 120
  influence over emigrants 75
literature, early Islamic 34–5, 36
low-intensity warfare 4
Luhmann, Niklas 110

McKinley, William (US President)
  139–40
Madrasat al-Sunnah language
  school in Cairo 47, 50
Maghreb region 108, 112n, 116,
  188
Mahdist movement (Sudan) 103
Mahmoody, Betty, *Not Without
  My Daughter* 19
Mahmud II, Sultan 46, 103
Marquardsen, Elsa (Elsa Sophia
  von Kamphöven) 54
masculinity, of Oriental culture
  34
Mashreq region 112n
masses, image of 15–17
al-Mawardi 94
al-Mawdudi, Abu al-Ala 89–91
May, Karl, German novelist 41
media
  portrayal of Islam as threat
    117–18, 146
  stereotyped views of Islam 7–8
Mernissi, Fatima 14–15
Middle East
  criticism of West 28
  importance to West 116, 126
  potential for conflict in 120–3,
    140–1
  Western ignorance of 7, 24
  *see also* Islamic countries;
    Orient
Mies, Maria 87
migration 1, 16, 72–6, 116
  effect on religious groupings
    74
  *see also* immigrants
Miller, Judith 131, 134–5

modernisation
   in 19th-century Ottoman
      empire 42–7
   associated with secularism 72
   as European 57–8
   rejected by fundamentalism
      84–5
modernity, perfected in Islam
   60–1, 68n
Mommsen, Katherina 35
Morocco 120
Muawia, first Umayyad caliph 96
Mu'awiyah ibn Abu Sufyan 91
Muhammad Ali Pasha, viceroy of
   Egypt 47, 50–1, 103
Muhammad, the Prophet, and
   blasphemy 78, 80–1n
Mujahidin (Afghanistan) 128
Muslim Brotherhood 64, 85, 90,
   91, 92, 104–7
   Israeli support for 128
   schism 108–9

an-Nabhani 90
an-Nadwi, Abu al-Hasan Ali 61
Najibullah, President of
   Afghanistan 128, 129
Napoleon Bonaparte, invasion of
   Egypt (1798) 21, 37–8, 57
Nasser, Gamal Abd al-, and
   Egyptian nationalism 87,
   102, 106
nationalism
   diversification within 108
   and popular Islam 87
   and religion 111–12n
   rise of Islamic 71–2
   *see also* Arab nationalism
*New Republic* (American
   magazine) 9, 10
*New York Times* 135–6
*New York Times Magazine* 131
*Newsweek* (American magazine)
   128, 130
North Africa 107
   Islamic influence in national-
      ism 100

nuclear weapons 1, 3, 124,
   135–9, 142
Numeiri, Jaffar al- 94, 97, 107

oil 1, 14, 116
   Iraqi threat to West's supplies
      of 124–5
Orient
   concept of 32–3, 41
   as dreamworld 33–7
   as feminine 39–40
   'real' 38, 40–1
   *see also* Islamic countries;
      Middle East
Othman, third caliph 95, 96
Ottoman empire
   19th-century modernisation
      42–7
   and Arab nationalism 104
   diplomatic links with France
      43–5
   and French Revolution 32,
      42–5
   Greek conflict with 38–9
   as threat to Europe 33
   *see also* Turkey

Pakistan 108, 142
   application of Sharia 94
   as Islamic nation state 98
   Jama'at-i-Islam network 75,
      107
   US support for Zia 129–30
Palestine 3, 99
Palestine Liberation Organization
   (PLO) 128
Palestinian conflict 108, 121
poetry 34–5, 36
political religion
   historicisation of 89–91
   Islamic movement in crisis
      107–11
   and popular religious
      movements 85–6
   as secularised politics 82–3
   trends in 84
polygamy 53

popular religion 85, 87, 88, 102, 108
population explosion, in Middle East 15
postmodernism 58, 59
poverty, Western fear of 25

Qutb, Sayyid 90, 91, 104

racism, growth of 29
radicalism
  in Islamic organisations 108
  social profile of activists 109–10
al-Rantisi, Abdel Aziz 158
Rashid Rida, Muhammad 104
Reagan, Ronald (US President), on Zia 129
religion
  and French revolution 44–5
  function of 110
  and ideology 83, 156
  and oppression of women 20, 156
  and secularisation 82–3, 111n
  should be discounted in international relations 155–6
  and terrorism 143–4
  in US politics 139–40, 143, 155–6
  Western fear of 21–2, 25–7, 118, 134
  *see also* Islam (religion); political religion; popular religion
religious conservatism 86, 88
Rifa'a al-Tahtawi, Egyptian reformer 48–50
Rodinson, Maxime 86
Rushdie, Salman, *The Satanic Verses* 75, 77–80

Sadat, Muhammad Anwar 94, 102, 106, 110
Saddam Hussein
  threat to oil markets 124–5
  use of jihad 9, 133, 140

Saint-Simonist utopian socialism 40
al-Sanhuri 93
Sanussi movement (Libya) 103
Saudi Arabia
  financial power of 65, 66, 74, 97, 117
  fundamentalist constitution 94
  Islamic Conference Organisation (1966) 102
  religious intolerance in 130
  US support for 130
Second World War 71
secularisation, and political religion 82–3, 158
Selim III, Sultan 43, 44, 45, 103
separation of powers, in Islamic politics 64
Shanizade, Ottoman reformer 46, 47, 56n
Sharia (Islamic law) 62, 90–1, 95
  application of 93–4
  women's position in 19
Shari'ati, Ali 61
Shiite fundamentalism 117, 128
  and terrorism 132–5, 143
Shiite Muslims 141–2
Sivan, Emmanuel 102
social profile of activists 109–10
Somalia 121
sovereignty, in Islamic politics 63–4
Soviet Union
  in Afghanistan 127–8, 142
  Islam as buffer against 126–31
  role in Middle East 122, 123
  *see also* Commonwealth of Independent States
students, as activists 109–10
Sudan 103, 108, 121
  application of Sharia 94, 107
  Muslim Brotherhood in 106
Suez Canal 51
Sunna (words and deeds of the Prophet) 90, 93
Sunni Muslims 141
  terrorism by 133

Syria 99, 103, 134
  Muslim Brotherhood in 106,
    107
  and origins of Arab national-
    ism 100

Tadjikistan, civil war 121
Takfir wa-al-hirjah, schismatic
    group 109
*Tales from a Thousand and One
    Nights* (Galland) 34
*Taqiyah* (concealment of faith)
    141
terrorism 132–5, 143–4, 153n
  policies against 4, 134
  theology of 93–5
Third World
  military threat from 137–8
  Western fear of 25
Tibi, Bassam 2–3, 16, 87–8
  on Iran's foreign policy 141–3
*Time* (American magazine) 9, 118
Tophoven, Rolf, on terrorism
    132–5
Tunisia 108, 120
al-Turabi, Hasan 111
Turkey
  historical links with Europe 33
  Kurds in 120
  nationalism in 99
  relations with Iran 141
  rivalry with Arabic Muslims 75
  *see also* Kurds; Ottoman empire

Umayyid dynasty (Andalusia) 96
*ummah* (to mean modern nation)
    98, 101
United Nations 3, 22
United States of America
  and Afghanistan 128–9
  Islamic hatred of 110–11, 118
  Islamic immigrants 10, 26
  media views of Islam 7–8, 118

origins of fundamentalism in
    12, 84
  and Pakistan 129–30
  policies in Middle East 123–6,
    131
  use of religion in politics
    139–40
*US News and World report*
    (magazine) 118

Vienna, Turkish sieges of 33, 34

*Wahhabism* fundamentalist
    doctrine 94, 103
West, the
  assumption of superiority
    20–3, 146–7, 149–50, 154
  double standards 3, 157–8
  and nuclear weapons 136–7
  periods of conflict with Islam
    71, 148
  policy in Middle East 116, 143,
    144–50
  role in Middle East 122–3
  use of fundamentalism 130–1
  view of Islam 116, 131–2, 145
  *see also* Europe, United States
Western culture, pervasiveness of
    14–15, 28
Westernisation, equated with
    modernity 57–8, 87
Wilhelm II, Kaiser of Germany 52
women
  German view of 53–4
  oppression of 18–20, 157–8
  veiling 17–18
world revolution, threat of 1

Zia ul-Haq, president of Pakistan
    94, 97, 107, 129–30
Zionism 98
  *see also* Israel; Judaism
Ziya Pasha 51